# Christmas Memories

By

Jeannine Browning

Jeannine B. Browning
8552 Sylvan Dr.
Melbourne, FL 32904-2426



First Printing 5000 copies June 2001

ISBN: 0-9710006-0-3

Printed in the USA by
WIMMER
The Wimmer Companies
Memphis

For my precious...

With love from

# Christmas Memories

Jeannine Elizabeth Brown Browning is the author of Christmas Memories, as well as *Sand In My Shoes, Florida Fixin's* and *Kids at Work* cookbooks.

Jeannine was born in Webster, Florida. She is the 4th generation of her family born in Webster. Webster is a very small town in Sumter County, which is 50 miles west of Orlando, Florida. Jeannine is married to George Browning, her college sweetheart. They have four great children and eight wonderful grandchildren.

Jeannine grew up in a family where her mother and grandmother were truly wonderful cooks, and this love for cooking good food was passed on to Jeannine. Jeannine has also passed this love of cooking good food to her children.

*"Precious"*

*"Darlin'"*

*I have collected and loved angels for 25 plus years. Just to look at them makes me happy. Needless to say, I have many angels in our home.*

*In the early years I bought a few. Since then, they have all been given to me by family and friends, as gifts of love. My husband, George, has given me most of the angels in my collection.*

*Several angels were passed down to me from my Mama (my grandmother Brown). Those are very precious to me.*

*Because I love angels and because they make most people happy, you will find many angels in this cookbook...nice angels, naughty angels, happy or sad angels...all waiting to say that they are watching over you, and love you.*

*Enjoy "Precious" and "Darlin'", my twin little angels.*

# Table of Contents

My heart is filled with Christmas love,
For all my family and friends to see.
What better way to celebrate the birth of Christ,
Than on my bended knee?

## Christmas Memories is dedicated to...

My best friend, Leah Casper. She loves me, supports me, encourages me and understands me...always.

My precious sister, Colleen Barton. My love for her is so deep it cannot be measured.

My wonderful friend, Rosemary Brofos. Rosemary is the talented artist for Christmas Memories. She has added excitement and encouragement to every step of this book.

My deepest thanks to my family and friends for sharing some of their favorite recipes with me for Christmas Memories.

Colleen Brown Barton

Dennis Barton

Glenna Bressette

Sandy Breitmeier

Rosemary Brofos

Ginny Browning

Leah Casper

Julie Casper Clifton

Elizabeth Guth

Colleen Browning Hunter

Tricia Browning Mast

Karl McGinty

Leona Schoff

# All My Cousins

# "All My Cousins"

This section is dedicated to all my cousins.
Many of them contributed their favorite recipes for
*Christmas Memories.*
I have been blessed to have so many wonderful cousins!
They are some of the best people on this earth.
I love them all.

Sue Bobbitt Adams, David Bobbitt, Deborah Bobbitt, James Bobbitt, Johnny Bobbitt, Charles Carpenter, Kathrene Bobbitt Collins, Susan Bobbitt Cook, Frances Bobbitt Davis, Jane Wilkerson Harring, Betsy Bobbitt Lackey, Jane Warnock McElyea, Donna Bobbitt Moschello, Lydia Wilkerson Pettus, Rose Wilkerson Sturgeon, Martha Carpenter Swarengen, Margaret Bobbitt Tarlton, Nancy Bobbitt Taylor, C. G. Wagstaff, Charles Wilkerson, George Wilkerson, and Carol Bobbitt Wright.

# Apple Cake

**Cake**

- 3 *cups unsifted all-purpose flour*
- 1 *teaspoon baking soda*
- 1 *teaspoon salt*
- 3 *cups diced raw apples, peeled*
- 1 *cup chopped nuts (walnuts or pecans)*
- 1½ *cups oil*
- 2 *cups sugar*
- 3 *eggs, slightly beaten*
- 2 *teaspoons black walnut flavoring*

Sift together flour, baking soda and salt. Coat apples and nuts with a small amount of flour. Blend oil, sugar, eggs, flavoring and flour mixture. Fold in apples and nuts. Bake in greased and floured tube pan at 325° for 1 hour and 20 minutes. Cool.

**Icing**

- 1 *cup brown sugar*
- 1 *stick margarine*
- ¼ *cup milk*

Mix icing ingredients together. Bring to a boil. Boil for approximately 5 minutes until it begins to thicken. Cool slightly and spread on top and sides of cake.

## Baked Chicken Breast

- *6 skinless, boneless chicken breast halves*
- *3 slices Swiss or American cheese, each cut in half*
- *1 can cream of chicken soup*
- *6 thin tomato slices*
- *2 tablespoons margarine, melted*
- *½ cup herb seasoned stuffing mix, crushed*
- *Hot, cooked rice*

Place chicken in 3-quart oblong baking dish. Top with cheese. Stir soup and spread over cheese, top with tomato. Combine margarine and stuffing, sprinkle over tomato. Bake at 400° for 25 minutes or until chicken is no longer pink. Serve over rice. Makes 6 servings.

The love we show,
The happiness we share,
Bring joy to all we know
And contentment to those who care.

# Bar-B-Q Meatballs

**Meatballs**

2 *pounds ground beef, lean*
1 *package dry onion soup mix*
2 *eggs*
1 *cup seasoned dry breadcrumbs*
½ *teaspoon garlic powder*

Mix ground beef, onion soup, eggs, breadcrumbs and garlic powder. Roll into balls. Bake in shallow pan at 350° for 20 to 30 minutes or until brown.

**Barbecue Sauce**

1 *(18 ounce) barbecue sauce*
¼-½ *cup honey*
8-10 *drops Tabasco sauce*

Mix and pour over meatballs. Serve warm in chafing dish or can be frozen until needed.

## Broccoli, Cauliflower and Cheese Bake

- 2 *packages frozen broccoli*
- 1 *package frozen cauliflower*
- 1 *can cream of celery soup*
- 1 *small jar Cheese Whiz*
- 1 *can French fried onion rings*

Prepare broccoli and cauliflower as directed. Drain and place in a 1½ to 2-quart casserole dish. Combine soup (no milk) and Cheese Whiz. Heat until smooth and creamy, stirring often. Pour over vegetables and mix lightly. Cover with onion rings and bake at 325° for 20 to 25 minutes or until bubbly.

Create special memories for your grandchildren. Have a picture taken of you and each grandchild. Have two copies made, keeping one for yourself and giving the other (already framed) to that precious grandchild. It will become even more meaningful over the years.

# Cheese Sandwich Soufflés

*Mustard*
8 *slices whole-wheat bread*
1 *tomato, sliced (optional)*
½ *cup grated cheese (may use more to taste)*
2 *eggs, beaten*
2½ *cups milk*
1 *teaspoon dried basil*

Preheat oven to 350°. Spread equal amounts of mustard over 4 slices of bread. Arrange tomatoes next. Sprinkle with grated cheese. Top with the last 4 slices of bread. Beat together the eggs, milk and seasoning. Pour this over the bread and let stand 30 minutes. I also baste the bread frequently with the egg mixture. Bake for 40 to 45 minutes or until the milk mixture is set.

# Cheesecake Cookies

**Crumb Topping**

- *⅓ cup butter*
- *⅓ cup packed dark brown sugar*
- *1 cup all-purpose flour*
- *½ cup finely chopped walnuts*

Cream butter with sugar. Add flour and walnuts a little at a time. Mix well. Save 1 cup of crumbs for topping. Press remaining crumbs in bottom of 8-inch square pan. Bake at 350° for 12 minutes until lightly brown.

**Cheesecake Filling**

- *¼ cup sugar*
- *1 (8 ounce) package cream cheese, softened*
- *1 egg*
- *2 tablespoons milk*
- *1 tablespoon lemon juice*
- *½ teaspoon vanilla*

Blend sugar with cream cheese in small mixing bowl until smooth. Add egg, milk, lemon juice and vanilla; beat well. Spread over baked crust. Sprinkle with reserved crumb mixture. Bake at 350° for 25 minutes or until a knife inserted in filling comes out clean. Refrigerate.

## Chicken Casserole

- 3 *cups bite-sized cooked chicken*
- 1 *package Uncle Ben's long grain and wild rice*
- 1 *can cream of celery soup*
- 1 *small jar chopped pimento*
- 1 *medium onion, minced fine*
- 1 *can French style green beans, drained (or other vegetable(s) you might like)*
- 1 *cup mayonnaise*
- 1 *can water chestnuts, drained and sliced*
- 1 *cup chicken broth*

**Topping**

*1½ cups grated cheese*
*Salt and pepper to taste*
*Breadcrumbs*
*Red pepper (optional)*

Mix all together in large casserole. Top with 1½ cups or more of grated cheese and maybe a few breadcrumbs. Bake at 350° for 40 minutes.

The greatest gift you can give your spouse or your children and grandchildren is YOU.
Make time to spend quality time with those you love, and those who love you.

# Chiles Rellenos

- 1 *(#2) can California green chiles, about 18 chiles*
- 1 *pound Monterey Jack cheese cut ½-inch wide, ½-inch thick and 1-inch shorter than the chile*
- ½ *cup all-purpose flour (about)*

Drain canned chiles, remove seeds and stuff with the cheese stick. Roll each chile in flour to coat all over; gently shake off excess.

**Puffy Coating**

- 9 *eggs, separated*
- 1 *tablespoon water*
- 6 *tablespoons all-purpose flour*
- ½ *teaspoon salt*
- ½ *cup sharp Cheddar cheese, grated*
- *Salad oil*
- *Salsa Sauce*

Separate 9 eggs. Beat whites until they form soft peaks. Beat yolks with 1 tablespoon water, 6 tablespoons all-purpose flour, and ¼ teaspoon salt until thick and creamy; fold into whites. Heat about 1½-inches of salad oil in a wide frying pan over medium heat. Dip stuffed chiles into the fluff batter, place gently into hot oil. When bottoms are golden brown, gently turn using a spatula and fork, and cook other side. Drain on paper towels. Serve with hot (temperature) salsa sauce and cheese melted on top. I prepare the whole can and freeze the rellenos and microwave when I want to serve.

# Chinese Chicken

- ¼ *cup vegetable or corn oil*
- 1 *pound skinless, boneless chicken breast - cut in strips*
- 1 *medium/large onion, chopped*
- 2 *cloves garlic, chopped*
- 1 *cup each- broccoli, cauliflower, carrots*
- 1 *cup chicken broth - fat removed (chill till fat jells and skim off)*
- ⅔ *cup water*
- ⅓ *cup light soy sauce*
- 2 *tablespoons cornstarch*
- 2 *cups cooked rice*

Heat oil - medium/high. Quick fry chicken, remove to drain on paper towel. Lower heat to medium and sauté onion and garlic. Add vegetables and broth. Bring to boil - cover - cook 5 minutes. Combine water, soy sauce and cornstarch in measuring cup. Add to vegetables - stir until thickened. Return chicken - cover - cook 5 minutes. Serve over rice.

# Chinese Meatballs

**Meatballs**

*1½ pounds hamburger*
*¾ cup rolled oats*
*1 cup sliced water chestnuts, drained and chopped**
*1 egg, slightly beaten*
*1 tablespoon soy sauce*
*½ teaspoon garlic salt*
*½ onion, chopped*
*¼ teaspoon salt*

Mix meatball ingredients and form into small balls. Brown and drain off fat.

**Sauce**

*1 (8½ ounce) can crushed pineapple, drain and save juice*
*1 cup brown sugar*
*2 tablespoons cornstarch*
*1 cup beef bouillon*
*2 tablespoons soy sauce*
*½ cup red wine vinegar*
*⅓ chopped green pepper*

Drain pineapple. Mix pineapple juice and brown sugar with cornstarch. Put in saucepan, gradually adding remaining liquids. Cook, stirring until thickened. Add pineapple, green pepper and meatballs. Simmer 30 minutes. Serves 6.

**I chop ½ of the water chestnuts for meatballs and use the remaining slices in the sauce.*

## Chocolate Mound Balls

- 1 *(14 ounce) package angel flake coconut*
- 1 *(8 ounce) cream cheese*
- 1 *pound powdered sugar*
- 2 *tablespoons water*
- *Chocolate chips*

Mix and shape into balls. Melt chocolate, dip balls in chocolate and lay on waxed paper until firm. Store in refrigerator.

# Chocolate Raspberry Cheesecake - Best Ever

- 2 *(3 ounce) packages cream cheese, softened (do not use fat reduced)*
- 1 *(14 ounce) can sweetened condensed milk*
- 1 *egg*
- 3 *tablespoons lemon juice*
- 1 *teaspoon vanilla*
- 1 *cup fresh or frozen raspberries (remove liquid)*
- 1 *ready-made chocolate pie crust*

Preheat oven to 350°. Beat cheese until light and fluffy. Add condensed milk then egg, lemon juice and vanilla. Beat together. It will begin to thicken. Arrange raspberries in bottom of pie shell. Pour cream cheese mixture over raspberries. Bake 30 to 35 minutes or until center is set. Use a toothpick to test. Cool cheesecake.

**Topping**

- ¼ *cup whipping cream*
- 2 *(1 ounce) squares semi-sweet baking chocolate*
- *Raspberries*

In a small saucepan add ¼ cup whipping cream. Add 2 squares (1 ounce each) semisweet baking chocolate. Over low heat stir until chocolate is smooth and thickened. Pour over cake. Spread out to cover the top evenly. Refrigerate. Just before serving add raspberries that are still frozen to the edge of the crust.

*Martha says this cheesecake is absolutely delicious.*

## Clam Spinach Alfredo Sauce

*1 package Alfredo sauce mix*
*1 package chopped frozen spinach*
*1 can minced or whole clams*
*Juice of 1 lemon*

Prepare Alfredo sauce following package directions. Thaw spinach and squeeze with hand to remove all water. Drain clams, discarding liquid. Add clams, spinach, and lemon juice to Alfredo sauce after it has finished cooking. Serve over pasta or spaghetti.

## Tuna and Canned Tomato Salad 2000

*1 can diced tomatoes, drained*
*1 tablespoon onion, minced*
*½ bell pepper, finely chopped*
*1 small can tuna packed in water, drained*
*1 cup celery, diced*
*1 tablespoon fresh sweet basil, finely chopped*
*Mayonnaise to moisten (or Thousand Island dressing)*

Combine and enjoy.

## Claudia's Chicken

2 *cups chicken breasts*
2 *cups sliced celery or 1 cup celery and 1 cup carrots (I prefer the mixture)*
2 *cups croutons (herb seasoned)*
¾-1 *cup mayonnaise (real)*
½ *cup slivered almonds*
2 *tablespoons lemon juice*
2 *teaspoons minced onion*
½ *teaspoon salt*
1 *cup Cheddar cheese*

Bake chicken (boneless breasts). Cube to make 2 cups or more. Mix together next 7 ingredients. Bake at 450° 10 to 15 minutes. Top with cheese.

*I use 1 package herb Stove Top dressing; just mix dressing herb packet contents to mixture. I prefer lemon zest - 1 teaspoon to replace lemon juice.*

# Cool Oven Pound Cake

- 1 *cup butter*
- ½ *cup solid shortening*
- 3 *cups sugar*
- 5 *eggs*
- 1 *tablespoon vanilla*
- 3 *cups all-purpose flour*
- 1 *teaspoon baking powder*
- 1 *cup milk, room temperature*

Cream butter, shortening, and sugar. Add eggs 1 at a time and beat well. Add vanilla. Combine flour and baking powder. Add alternately with milk, beginning and ending with flour. Preheat oven to 325°. Pour into a Bundt pan and bake for 1 hour, 15 minutes without opening oven door.

Reaching out and touching someone you love is probably more important to that person than you will ever know.

## Cranberry Cocktail Rounds

*2 large packages cream cheese*
*1 can whole-berry cranberry sauce*
*½ cup nuts*
*½ cup dried cranberries*
*1 loaf bread*

Soften cream cheese. Add enough cranberry sauce to soften cream cheese; cream. Add nuts and finely cut up dried cranberries. Cut bread into rounds. Spread with cream cheese mixture.

## Easy Peach Pie

3 *cups sliced peaches*
2 *eggs, beaten*
⅓ *cup flour*
⅔ *cup sugar*
2 *tablespoons butter*

Mix all the above together. Pour into a 9-inch unbaked pie shell. Bake 40 minutes at 400°.

What you DO,
is what you BELIEVE.
All the rest is JUST TALK.

# Festive Stuffing Balls

- *½ cup chopped onion*
- *½ cup chopped celery*
- *2 tablespoons butter*
- *1 (12 ounce) can white kernel corn, drained (fresh corn is best if you have it)*
- *1 (8 ounce) package seasoned stuffing mix*
- *½ teaspoon salt*
- *¼ teaspoon pepper*
- *½ teaspoon crushed marjoram*
- *2 eggs*
- *1 cup milk*
- *½ cup melted butter*

Sauté onion and celery in butter in saucepan until tender, stirring frequently. Add corn, stuffing mix, seasonings, eggs and milk: mix well. Shape into 1¼ to 1½-inch balls. Place in shallow 9x13-inch or 10-inch round pan: pour melted butter over stuffing balls. Bake uncovered, in preheated 375° oven for 20 minutes. Delicious served with leftover turkey or chicken gravy. Makes 25 to 28 stuffing balls.

## Gingersnaps

- ¾ *cup shortening*
- 1 *cup brown sugar, firmly packed*
- 1 *egg*
- 4 *tablespoons molasses*
- 2¼ *cups flour*
- 2 *teaspoons baking soda*
- ¼ *teaspoon salt*
- 1 *teaspoon ground cloves*
- 1 *teaspoon ground cinnamon*
- 1½ *teaspoons ginger*
- ½ *cup granulated sugar*

Cream shortening and brown sugar. Add egg and molasses. Combine flour, baking soda and spices. Add to brown sugar mixture. Mix well. Roll into balls. Dip tops in granulated sugar. Bake at 325° for 12 to 15 minutes.

*Watch it, they burn easily on the bottoms.*

Consider each day
as a precious gift from God,
to be enjoyed as fully as possible.

## Gorgeous Fries

*6 baking potatoes*
*½ cup butter (1 stick)*
*Onion salt (to taste)*
*1 (8 ounce) package Parmesan cheese*
*Paprika*

Cut potatoes into ½-inch wide sticks. Put in ice water for ½ hour. Drain and dry and place on cookie sheet. Slice butter and scatter over potatoes. Sprinkle onion salt to taste. Bake at 350° for 1 hour. Toss with spatula every 10 to 15 minutes. Five minutes before removing, sprinkle with Parmesan cheese and paprika. Serves 6 to 8.

# Ham Rolls

- *4 packages small dinner rolls*
- *1½ pounds thinly sliced ham*
- *½ pound Monterey Jack cheese, grated*
- *2 sticks butter, melted*
- *2 tablespoons poppy seeds*
- *1 small onion, grated*
- *1 tablespoon Worcestershire sauce*
- *3-4 tablespoons mustard (Dijon)*
- *Salt and pepper to taste*

Freeze rolls in package, then remove from package and slice horizontally. Mix all remaining ingredients together, except ham. Spread evenly on rolls, top and bottom, with pastry brush. Put ham on bottom half of rolls, then place top of rolls on ham. Warm immediately OR freeze until ready to eat. Slice as desired.

# Lemon Pie

**Crust**

*15 crushed vanilla wafers*
*¼ cup softened butter*
*½ cup sugar*
*Vanilla wafers*

Mix first 3 ingredients and press in bottom of pie shell. Place additional vanilla wafers around sides.

**Filling**

*3 egg yolks (save whites)*
*½ cup lemon juice*
*1 can sweetened condensed milk*

Blend eggs yolks and lemon juice. Slowly add condensed milk. Pour into pie crust/shell and bake in preheated 375° oven for 7 minutes. Remove and let cool.

**Meringue**

*3 egg whites*
*½ teaspoon cream of tartar*
*½ cup sugar*
*Pinch of salt*

Whip egg whites and cream of tartar, adding sugar 1 tablespoon at a time. Add a pinch of salt. Whip until stiff. Spoon over pie. Place under the broiler with the oven door open until meringue turns light tan. Refrigerate 2 hours before serving.

## Lima Beans

*4 cans lima beans (I use freshly cooked butter beans)*
*1 green pepper, grated*
*½ cup fresh parsley, no stems*
*1 teaspoon salt*
*1 teaspoon MSG*
*2 tablespoons sugar*
*4 cloves minced garlic*
*½ cup olive oil*

Mix all ingredients and bake at 325° for at least 1½ hours.

## Little Party Pizzas

- *1 pound grated sharp Cheddar cheese (or 1 pound mixed grated cheese)*
- *1 small can tomato sauce*
- *½ cup oil (I like ¼ cup vegetable and ¼ cup olive oil)*
- *½ teaspoon Italian seasoning*
- *1 finely chopped onion*
- *1 small can chopped black olives*
- *1 finely chopped bell pepper*
- *Finely chopped pepperoni (optional)*
- *Fresh mushrooms (optional)*
- *Crumbled Italian sausage (optional)*
- *English muffins*

Mix the ingredients listed above and store in a covered container in the refrigerator. When your guests become hungry, pull out the mixture. Cut English muffins in half. Toast the inside half of each muffin under the broiler or toast lightly in a toaster. Spread each muffin half with a heavy coating of the pizza mixture. Bake in a 350° oven for approximately 10 minutes or until bubbly and lightly brown. Check them often as they burn quickly.

## Mashed Potato Casserole

*8-10 medium potatoes, peeled and sliced*
*Salt and pepper to taste*
*1 (8 ounce) package cream cheese, softened*
*2 eggs, lightly beaten*
*2 tablespoons all-purpose flour*
*2 tablespoons minced parsley*
*2 tablespoons minced chives or grated onion*
*1 (3½ ounce) can French fried onion for topping*

Peel, slice, then boil potatoes until tender. Drain. Put in large mixing bowl and using an electric hand mixer beat until smooth. Add salt, pepper and cream cheese. Then add eggs, flour, parsley and chives. Turn into buttered 2-quart casserole. Spread slightly crushed onions over top and bake uncovered at 325° for 30 to 40 minutes until puffy. Casserole can be frozen.

## Mexican Mocha Balls

- 1 *cup butter*
- ½ *cup sugar*
- 1 *teaspoon vanilla*
- 2 *cups all-purpose flour*
- ¼ *cup cocoa*
- 1 *teaspoon instant coffee*
- ¼ *teaspoon salt*
- 1 *cup walnuts, chopped*
- ½ *cup maraschino cherries, chopped*
- *Powdered sugar*

Cream butter with sugar and vanilla. In a small bowl mix flour, cocoa, coffee, salt and walnuts. Add to butter mixture. Stir well. Add cherries. Chill for at least 2 hours. Roll into small balls and bake for about 10 to 12 minutes in 325° or 350° oven depending on how hot your oven gets. Don't overcook. Roll in powdered sugar.

# Mother Mc's Dark Fruit Cake

2 *cups sugar*
1 *pound softened butter*
4 *cups all-purpose flour*
10 *eggs*
1 *teaspoon baking soda (mix in 2 tablespoons warm water)*
1 *(8 ounce) jar mincemeat*
4 *ounces brandy (optional)*
1 *pound raisins (white or dark)*
1 *pound dates*
1 *pound candied cherries, cut into halves*
1 *pound candied pineapple (can be cut or left whole)*
2 *cups pecans, coarsely chopped*

Grease and lightly flour 2 tube pans. In extra large bowl mix sugar and butter. Add flour, eggs and baking soda alternately to the sugar/butter mixture. Add mincemeat and brandy. Gradually mix in candied fruits and nuts. Pour into tube pans and bake in preheated 300° oven for 2½ hours. When cakes are completely cooled, turn tube pans upside down and place cakes on cake racks, plate or tray. Be sure to cover tightly with aluminum foil. These keep well for several weeks.

## Mystery Cookies

- 2 *cups light or dark brown sugar (1 16-ounce box)*
- 1¼ *cups all-purpose flour*
- 1 *teaspoon baking powder*
- 1 *egg, lightly beaten*
- 1 *cup melted butter*
- 1 *teaspoon vanilla*
- 1 *cup pecans, chopped (or 2 cups peanuts or M & M's)*
- *Pinch of salt*
- *Powdered sugar*

Mix sugar, flour and baking powder. Pour into egg and add other ingredients. Bake in middle of oven for 45 minutes or until batter falls. Cut into squares. Let cool. When absolutely cold, roll in powdered sugar, if desired. Everyone loves mystery cookies. The secret is in the melted butter.

*Beware of overcooking or cookies will be like bricks.*

## Pecan Balls

- 1 *stick butter*
- 3 *tablespoons powdered sugar*
- 1 *cup sifted all-purpose flour*
- 1 *cup pecans, chopped*

Cream butter and sugar. Stir in flour and pecans. Chill for about an hour. Shape into balls. Bake at 350° for about 10 to 12 minutes. Don't overbake. Cool, then roll in powdered sugar.

Work on your attitude.
Make sure it is as positive
and happy as possible.
SMILE, SMILE, SMILE!

## Pecan Pie

- *4 tablespoons all-purpose flour*
- *1 cup sugar*
- *4 tablespoons margarine, melted*
- *5 medium eggs*
- *½ teaspoon salt*
- *2 teaspoons vanilla*
- *1 bottle Karo white syrup*
- *1½ cups pecans*
- *2 frozen 9-inch pie shells (not deep)*

Mix flour and sugar well. Melt margarine and add to flour/sugar mixture, mixing well. Beat eggs and add to mixture. Mix well. Add salt, vanilla and Karo syrup. Mix well. Add pecans and stir well. Pour into unbaked pie shells. Bake in preheated 350° oven for 35 to 45 minutes. Shake to see if pie is done.

If you love someone,
SHOW IT!

# Pumpkin-Sweet Potato Pie

**Pie Filling**

1 *cup pumpkin*
1 *cup grated raw sweet potatoes*
1 *cup coconut, ground fine*
1 *cup sugar*
2 *tablespoons all-purpose flour*
½ *cup milk*
½ *stick margarine*
2 *eggs*
1 *teaspoon vanilla*
1 *teaspoon cinnamon*
1 *pie crust, unbaked*

Mix pie ingredients and pour into crust.

**Topping**

⅓ *cup brown sugar*
2 *tablespoons all-purpose flour*
½ *cup butter, chopped*

Top with ⅓ cup brown sugar and 2 tablespoons all-purpose flour. Dot with small amount of butter. Bake at 350° for about 40 minutes or until done. Makes 1 deep dish pie or double recipe and make 3 regular size pies.

## Sausage Casserole

*1½ pounds sausage (hot or mild)*
*8 slices trimmed white bread - cubed*
*1½ cups milk*
*9 eggs, beaten*
*1½ cups grated sharp cheese*
*Salt and pepper to taste*

Cook sausage; drain well. Grease a 9x13-inch pan. Line bottom with bread cubes. Put sausage on top. Mix milk with beaten eggs. Pour over sausage. Sprinkle with cheese. Bake at 350° for 30 minutes. Can be refrigerated 2 or 3 hours or overnight. Serves 8 or 10.

*I like to use this one for Sunday brunch or when I'm having overnight guests.*

# Sausage/Broccoli Quiche

- *1 (9-inch) pie shell*
- *4 Brown & Serve breakfast sausages*
- *1 cup chopped broccoli (fresh or frozen)*
- *1 cup shredded Cheddar cheese*
- *4 large or 5 medium eggs*
- *1 cup half & half*
- *¼ teaspoon prepared mustard*
- *Nutmeg*

Bake pie shell (approximately 5 minutes according to directions). Set aside. Brown sausage, cool, slice in sections and place in bottom of pie shell. Steam or microwave broccoli - 2 minutes. Place in pie shell. Sprinkle cheese. In small mixing bowl - beat eggs, stir in half & half and mustard - pour over sausage and broccoli. Sprinkle with nutmeg. Bake in preheated over at 375° for 35 to 40 minutes. Test with toothpick.

# Stuffed Fish Fillets

*Light cooking spray*
1 *tablespoon light margarine*
2 *tablespoons minced onion*
½ *cup chopped mushrooms*
1 *(10 ounce) package frozen spinach (thawed and squeezed dry)*
1 *tablespoon lemon juice*
1½ *pounds flounder or sole (approximately 4 fillets)*

Spray sauté pan with cooking spray, melt 1 tablespoon margarine. Sauté onion and mushrooms over medium heat until onions are clear. Add spinach - cook 5 minutes. Rinse and dry fillets. Cover each with ¼ spinach mix. Roll fillets with seam side down and place in microwave cooking dish (approximately 6x9-inch).

**Light Cheese Sauce**
2 *tablespoons light margarine*
2 *tablespoons flour*
¼ *teaspoon chopped tarragon*
⅛ *teaspoon white pepper*
1 *cup skim milk*
¼ *cup low fat or fat-free Swiss cheese (shredded)*
¼ *cup low fat Parmesan cheese*
¼ *cup white wine*

In small saucepan melt 2 tablespoons light margarine. Add flour, tarragon and pepper. Slowly add milk and bring to medium heat - stir constantly. As sauce begins to thicken, add Parmesan and Swiss cheese- stir until melted. Add wine and stir. Pour sauce over fish fillets. Cover with plastic wrap or microwave cover. Microwave on high 6 to 8 minutes or until fish is opaque. In conventional oven bake at 325° for 20 to 25 minutes.

## Sweet Potato Pie

2 *cups baked, sweet potatoes, mashed*
2 *eggs, beaten*
1½ *cups sugar*
1 *stick margarine, melted*
1 *small can evaporated milk*
1 *small package instant vanilla pudding mix*
1 *teaspoon vanilla flavoring*

Mix all ingredients together and pour into 2 pie shells. Bake at 450° for 20 minutes, then reduce heat to 300° and continue baking until knife inserted in center comes out clean, approximately 30 minutes.

## Tea Punch

- ¼ *cup instant tea (not mix)*
- ½ *cup lemonade mix*
- ½ *cup white grape juice*
- 1½ *cups sugar*

Mix all ingredients and add water to make 1 gallon. Refrigerate at least 2 days before serving.

Remember to say
"I love you"
at least once a day to all you love.

## Two-Layer Cake

- 2 1/8 *cups (or 2 cups + 2 tablespoons) sifted, self-rising flour*
- 1 1/2 *cups sugar*
- 1/2 *cup shortening (Crisco)*
- 1 *cup milk*
- 1 *teaspoon flavoring (vanilla, almond or lemon)*
- 2 *eggs, unbeaten*

Stir flour, sugar and shortening. Add milk and flavoring, then eggs. Beat vigorously 200 or more strokes. Batter will be thin. Bake in 2 (8-inch) greased and floured pans at 350° for 30 to 35 minutes. Cover with your favorite icing.

## Unfried French Fries

4 *potatoes*
2 *large egg whites*
1 *tablespoon Cajun spice*

Preheat oven to 400°. Spray pan with vegetable oil. Peel and slice potatoes into French fries. Coat potatoes in egg whites and Cajun spice. Put on bottom shelf of oven. Space single layer. Bake 40 to 45 minutes. Turn every 6 to 8 minutes.

# Veggie Chili

*1 onion, diced*
*½ bell pepper, diced*
*½ teaspoon minced garlic*
*3 cans stewed tomatoes*
*1 package tofu crumbles*
*¼ teaspoon ground cumin*
*½ teaspoon chili powder*
*¼ teaspoon salt*
*2 cans red or chili beans*

Spray pot with Pam or use a small amount of oil. Sauté onion, peppers and garlic in pot on medium heat until tender (maybe 5 minutes). Add stewed tomatoes, crumbles and seasonings. Increase heat to medium high until it begins to bubble. Simmer for about an hour (low heat, partially covered). Stir once in a while. Add beans. Taste and adjust seasonings as needed. Serve.

## Whipper Snappers

*1 (18½ ounce) package lemon cake mix*
*2 cups Cool Whip*
*1 egg*
*Grated lemon rind*
*Powdered sugar*

Mix first 4 ingredients together. Take 1 teaspoon and roll into a ball. Dip tops in powdered sugar. Bake on greased cookie sheet at 350° for 10 to 15 minutes.

## Zesty Deviled Chicken

- 3 *tablespoons butter*
- 1 *cup dry breadcrumbs*
- 1 *teaspoon sugar*
- 1 *teaspoon paprika*
- ¼ *teaspoon onion powder*
- 1 *egg*
- ¼ *cup prepared mustard*
- 1 *(2½ to 3 pound) fryer chicken, cut up and skinned*

Melt butter in a 12x8x2-inch baking dish. Set aside. Combine breadcrumbs, sugar, paprika, and onion powder in a shallow dish. Combine egg and mustard; brush evenly on chicken. Coat chicken with breadcrumb mixture and place in prepared dish. Bake at 400° for 25 minutes, turn chicken in baking dish. Bake an additional 20 minutes. Serves 4.

# Make Ahead Spinach Manicotti

- 1 *(15 ounce) container ricotta cheese*
- 1 *(10 ounce) package frozen spinach, chopped, thawed and squeezed dry*
- 1½ *cups mozzarella cheese, shredded*
- ¾ *cup Parmesan cheese, shredded*
- 1 *egg*
- ½ *tablespoon onion powder*
- 2 *tablespoons parsley, fresh and minced*
- ½ *teaspoon pepper*
- ⅛ *teaspoon garlic powder*
- 1½ *cups water*
- 2 *(28 ounce) jars spaghetti sauce with meat*
- 1 *(8 ounce) package manicotti shells, uncooked*

Combine ricotta cheese, spinach, 1 cup mozzarella cheese, ¼ cup Parmesan cheese, egg, parsley, pepper and onion powder. Combine spaghetti sauce and water. Spread 1 cup spaghetti sauce in ungreased 9x13-inch pan. Stuff uncooked shells with spinach mixture, arrange over sauce. Pour remaining sauce over shells. Sprinkle with remaining mozzarella and Parmesan cheeses. Cover and refrigerate overnight. Remove 30 minutes before baking. Uncover and bake at 350° for 40 to 50 minutes.

# Holiday Ham and Cheese Balls

- 3 *cups Bisquick baking mix*
- 2 *cups finely chopped baked ham*
- 2 *cups (16 ounces) Cheddar cheese, grated*
- ½ *cup Parmesan cheese*
- 2 *tablespoons parsley flakes*
- ¼-½ *teaspoon garlic or onion salt (optional)*
- 2-3 *teaspoons spicy mustard (according to taste)*
- ⅔-¾ *cup milk*
- *Pimento stuffed olives cut into halves*

Preheat oven to 350°. Mix all ingredients thoroughly. Shape into 1-inch balls. Wrap each ball around ½ of an olive then seal. Freeze on baking pan then place in plastic bags and return to freezer until needed, or bake for approximately 12 to 15 minutes or until brown. Do not over bake or they will be dry.

# Zucchini Bread

- *4 cups coarsely grated zucchini*
- *3 cups all-purpose flour*
- *2½ cups sugar*
- *1¼ cups vegetable oil*
- *4 eggs, beaten*
- *1 tablespoon plus 1 teaspoon vanilla*
- *1 tablespoon ground cinnamon*
- *1½ teaspoons salt*
- *1½ teaspoons baking soda*
- *½ teaspoon baking powder*
- *1 cup chopped nuts (optional)*

Heat oven to 325°. Generously grease bottoms only of 2 loaf pans, 9x5x3-inches. Blend all ingredients on low speed 1 minute, scraping bowl constantly. Beat on medium speed 1 minute. Pour into pans. Bake until wooden pick inserted in center comes out clean, 50 minutes to 1 hour. Cool 10 minutes: remove from pans. Cool completely. Makes 2 loaves.

*If using self-rising flour, omit salt, baking soda and baking powder.*

## Zucchini Bread

**Beat together**

3 *eggs*
2 *cups sugar*
1 *cup oil*
3 *teaspoons vanilla*
2 *cups zucchini, grated*

**Blend**

2¼ *cups all-purpose flour*
1 *teaspoon baking soda*
½ *teaspoon baking powder*
1 *tablespoon cinnamon*
1 *teaspoon salt*

Combine 2 mixtures. Put into 2 loaf pans. Bake 1 hour at 325°. Makes 2 loaves.

## Where Do You Buy "Scratch?"

*Submitted by Sue Adams*
*Author Unknown*

My mother never let me help much in the kitchen. As a result, my cooking ability was practically nonexistent when I got married. But I did remember Mother mentioning to her friends that she's made cakes, pies and other things from scratch. So my first priority after the honeymoon was to locate some scratch. With Mother's delicious cakes in mind, my first trip to the supermarket was to buy some scratch. I found the aisle that read "baking items." I spent a good 15 minutes looking at everything from vegetable oil, sugar, flour and chocolate, without seeing a sign of scratch. I was sure it wouldn't be with the pickles or the meat. I asked the clerk if they carried scratch. He looked at me funny and finally said, "You'll have to go to the store on the corner." When I got there, it turned out to be a feed store. I though it rather strange, but I decided cakes were feed. "Do you have scratch?" I asked the clerk. He asked me how much I wanted. I suggested a pound or two. His reply was, "How many chickens do you have? It only comes in 20 pound bags." I really didn't understand why he mentioned chickens, but I had heard Mother say she made some chicken casserole from scratch so I bought 20 pounds and hurried home.

My next problem was to find a recipe calling for scratch. I went through every single page of my lovely Better Homes and Garden Cookbook, given as a wedding present, looking for a recipe calling for scratch. There I was with 20 pounds of scratch and no recipe.

When I opened the scratch I had doubts that a beautiful fluffy cake would ever result from such a hard-looking ingredient. I hoped with the addition of liquids and heat, the result would be successful. I had no need to mention my problem to my husband as he suggested very early in our marriage he liked to cook and would gladly take over anytime. One day he made a pie and when I told him how good it was, he said he made it from scratch. That assured me it could be done.

Being a new bride is scary and when I found out he made pies, cakes and even lemon pudding from scratch...well, if he made all those things from scratch I was sure he had bought a 20-pound bag also. But I couldn't find where he stored it and I checked my supply...it was still full. At this point I was ready to give up because all the people knew about scratch except me.

I decided to try a different approach. One day when my husband was not doing anything, I said, "Honey, I wish you'd bake a cake." He got out the flour, eggs, milk and shortening, but not a sign of scratch. I watched him blend it together, pour it into a pan and slide it in the oven to bake. An hour later as we were eating the cake, I looked at him and smiled and said, "Honey, why don't we raise a few chickens."

# Gifts to Make & Share

# My Precious Mother

My Mother is the one
Who cared for me each day,
She is the precious one,
Who taught me to kneel and pray.

She cared for me when I was sick,
She loved me whether I was good or bad.
She is the most wonderful mother
Any child has ever had.

Jeannine Browning

Her children stand and bless her; so does her husband.
He praises her with these words:
"There are many fine women in the world,
but you are the best of them all."

Proverbs 31:28-29

# Banana Bread

- *1¼ cups all-purpose flour*
- *1 cup sugar*
- *½ teaspoon salt*
- *1 teaspoon baking soda*
- *½ vegetable oil*
- *3 small ripe bananas*
- *2 eggs*

Mix dry ingredients in bowl. Combine the oil and the dry ingredients with your (clean) fingers. Puree the bananas (or mash well with a fork) and add to the flour and oil along with the well-beaten eggs. Mix quickly, but don't over mix. Pour into a greased and floured 9x5x3-inch pan and bake at 350 degrees for 45 minutes or until inserted toothpick comes out clean.

*Other suggestions for this recipe. Instead of 3 small ripe bananas you can use ½ cup applesauce and ½ cup banana, or ½ cup canned pumpkin and ½ cup banana. You can also add raisins and/or chopped pecans or walnuts. Banana bread can also be sliced and spread with cream cheese or jam and butter.*

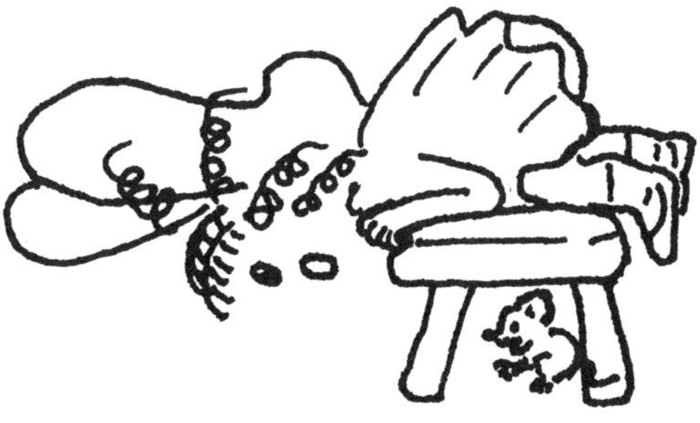

# Best Ever Lemon Pie

*1 baked 9-inch pie shell*
*1½ cups sugar*
*1½ cups water*
*½ teaspoon salt*
*½ cup cornstarch*
*⅓ cup water*
*4 egg yolks, slightly beaten*
*½ cup lemon juice*
*3 tablespoons butter*
*1 teaspoon grated lemon peel*

**Meringue**
*4 egg whites*
*¼ teaspoon salt*
*½ cup sugar*

Combine sugar, 1½ cups water and salt in saucepan; heat to boiling. Mix cornstarch and ⅓ cup water to make smooth paste; add to boiling mixture gradually, stirring constantly. Cook until thick and clear. Remove from heat. Combine egg yolks and lemon juice; stir into thickened mixture. Return to heat and cook, stirring constantly until mixture bubbles again. Remove from heat. Stir in butter and lemon peel. Cover and cool until lukewarm.

For meringue, add salt to egg whites. Beat until frothy. Gradually add ½ cup sugar, beating until glossy peaks are formed. Stir 2 rounded tablespoons of meringue into lukewarm filling. Pour filling into cool pie shell. Pile remaining meringue on top and spread lightly over filling, spreading evenly to edge of crust.

Bake in a slow oven (325°) about 15 minutes or until lightly browned. Cool on rack at least 1 hour before cutting.

## Black Forest Cheesecake

*1½ cups chocolate cookie crumbs*
*¼ cup butter, melted*

Combine crumbs and butter; blend well. Press into bottom and 1-inch up sides of a 9-inch springform pan.

*3 (8 ounce) packages cream cheese, softened*
*1½ cups sugar*
*4 eggs*
*⅓ cup cherry flavored liqueur*

Beat cream cheese with a mixer until fluffy, add sugar gradually, blending well. Add eggs, one at a time, mixing well. Add liqueur, continuing to beat until mixed. Spread into prepared crust and bake at 350° for 55 to 60 minutes or until set. Cool completely.

*4 (1 ounce) squares semi-sweet chocolate*
*½ cup sour cream*
*12 maraschino cherries with stems*

In the top of a double boiler, melt chocolate; allow to cool, then stir in sour cream. Spoon over top of cheesecake and chill thoroughly before serving. Slice and garnish each slice with a cherry.

## Blueberry Muffins

| | | | |
|---|---|---|---|
| 3 | *cups flour* | 1½ | *cups blueberries* |
| ¾ | *cup sugar* | 2 | *eggs* |
| 1 | *tablespoon baking powder* | ½ | *cup oil* |
| ¾ | *teaspoon salt* | 1⅛ | *cups milk* |

Combine flour, sugar, baking powder and salt. Stir in blueberries. Beat eggs, oil and milk together. Stir liquid into flour mixture just until moist. Spoon into greased muffin cups. Bake at 400° for 20 minutes. Makes 12 large muffins.

Look to the beauty of this day –
miracles are all around you!

## Butterscotch Brownies

*1½ cups all-purpose flour*
*2 teaspoons baking powder*
*½ cup margarine or butter*
*2 cups brown sugar, packed*
*2 eggs*
*1 teaspoon vanilla*
*1 cup pecans, chopped*

Grease and flour shallow, rectangular baking pan. Sift flour with baking powder. Melt butter carefully over low heat, add sugar and bring to a boil, stirring constantly. Remove from heat and cool to lukewarm. Drop in eggs, one at a time, mixing well. Stir in vanilla, flour mixture and nuts. Pour into baking pan. Bake at 350° for 30 to 35 minutes. Cool in pan, cut and serve.

# Chocolate Fruitcake

- 1 *cup butter or margarine*
- 6 *(1 ounce) squares semi-sweet chocolate*
- 1¼ *cups sugar*
- 3 *large eggs*
- 1 *cup all-purpose flour*
- ¼ *teaspoon salt*
- 1 *cup red candied cherries, cut in half*
- 1 *cup green candied pineapple, cut into ½-inch slices*
- ¾ *cup walnuts, coarsely chopped*
- ¾ *cup pecans, coarsely chopped*

Melt butter and chocolate in a heavy saucepan over low heat, stirring often. Remove from heat, and cool about 15 minutes. Stir in sugar. Add eggs, one at a time, stirring well after each addition. Add flour and salt (stirred together), stirring until blended. Stir in cherries, pineapple and nuts. Spoon mixture into 4 greased and floured 5x3x2-inch loaf pans, or spoon into one large tube pan (I use the tube pan). Bake at 350° for 35 minutes for loaf pans or 1½ hours for tube pan. Always check with a tester to determine when done. I use a colored, wooden toothpick to determine if cake is done. If you stick the toothpick near the center of the cake and the toothpick comes back clean, your cake is done. If the toothpick comes out with batter on it you need to cook for another 10 to 15 minutes and check again. Cool in pans on wire rack for 10 to 30 minutes. Remove when completely cool. Place cakes on serving dish until completely cool, then wrap in Saran Wrap or foil. When ready to eat, just slice and serve. Yum!

# Chocolate Pound Cake

- 1 *cup margarine*
- ½ *cup solid shortening*
- 3 *cups sugar*
- 5 *eggs, at room temperature*
- 3 *cups cake flour*
- ½ *teaspoon baking powder*
- ½ *teaspoon salt*
- ¼ *cup baking cocoa*
- 1 *cup whole milk*
- 1 *tablespoon vanilla*

Cream margarine and shortening with sugar; add eggs one at a time, beating until very light and fluffy. Sift flour, baking powder, salt and cocoa together. Blend dry ingredients into creamed mixture alternately with milk in small amounts, beating well after each addition. Add vanilla and stir well. Turn into greased 10-inch tube pan. Bake in 325° oven for 1 hour and 20 minutes or until done. Cool in pan for 15 minutes. Remove from pan by placing cake plate on top of cake and gently turning over. Cake should fall out of pan onto cake plate. When cool spread with Yummy Chocolate Frosting.

### Yummy Chocolate Frosting

- ¼ *cup margarine*
- 3 *squares unsweetened chocolate*
- 1 *(16 ounce) box confectioners' sugar*
- ½ *teaspoon vanilla*
- *Milk or heavy cream*

Melt margarine and chocolate in top of double boiler; stir until smooth. Blend in sugar and vanilla. Add small amount of milk or cream to get correct spreading consistency.

# Chocolate Sheet Cake

*1¼ cups butter or margarine*
*½ cup baking cocoa*
*1 cup water*
*2 cups unsifted all-purpose flour*
*1½ cups firmly packed brown sugar*
*1 teaspoon baking soda*
*1 teaspoon ground cinnamon*
*½ teaspoon salt*
*1 (14 ounce) can sweetened condensed milk*
*2 eggs*
*1 teaspoon vanilla*
*1 cup confectioners' sugar*
*1 cup pecans or walnuts, chopped*

Preheat oven to 350°. In small pot, melt 1 cup margarine and stir in ¼ cup cocoa, then water. Bring to a boil; remove from heat. In large mixer bowl combine flour, brown sugar, baking soda, cinnamon and salt. Add cocoa mixture, beat well. Stir in ½ cup condensed milk, eggs and vanilla. Pour into greased 15x10-inch pan. Bake 15 minutes or until cake springs back when lightly touched. In small pan, melt remaining ¼ cup butter; stir in remaining ¼ cup cocoa and condensed milk. Stir in confectioners' sugar and nuts. Spread over warm cake.

## Christmas Candy

*4 cups pecans, finely chopped*
*2 (16 ounce) boxes confectioners' sugar*
*1 (14 ounce) can sweetened condensed milk*
*1 stick butter, room temperature*
*1 (7 ounce) package coconut*
*Pinch of salt*
*1 teaspoon vanilla*
*1 (16 ounce) package chocolate candy kisses or 1 (12 ounce) package semi-sweet chocolate morsels*
*Paraffin, grated*

Mix pecans, sugar, milk, butter, coconut, salt and vanilla. Roll into small balls. Melt chocolate with a small to medium amount of paraffin. Stir until smooth. Roll balls in chocolate until well coated. Put on wax paper and place in refrigerator until firm.

## Christmas Cookies

*5½ cups all-purpose flour*
*2 cups sugar*
*3 eggs*
*1 cup butter or margarine*
*3 teaspoons baking powder*
*2 tablespoons milk*
*1 teaspoon nutmeg*
*½ teaspoon cloves*

Combine ingredients, mix well. Store in refrigerator for about a week in a tightly covered container. Roll out dough and cut with cookie cutters. Bake at 325° for 8 to 10 minutes. Cool, then ice and decorate. They will keep well for about a month.

## Christmas Fruit Bars

*1 stick butter or margarine*
*1 cup brown sugar, packed*
*1 tablespoon vanilla*
*2 eggs*
*½ pound candied cherries, cut into halves*
*½ pound candied pineapple, sliced*
*2 cups pecans*
*1 cup self-rising flour*

Grease and flour a 10x14-inch pan. Cream butter and brown sugar together. Add eggs, one at a time, mixing well after each. Add vanilla, then flour. Add pecans and candied fruit and mix well. Spoon batter into pan and use spoon to smooth batter. Bake in 325° oven for 1 hour.

If you allow someone
to make you angry, you have let
him/her conquer you.

## Cocoa Fudge

*⅔ cup baking cocoa*
*3 cups sugar*
*½ teaspoon salt*
*1½ cups whole milk*
*¼ cup butter or margarine*
*1 teaspoon vanilla*
*½ cup pecans, finely chopped*

Combine cocoa, sugar and salt in a 3-quart pan. Add milk gradually, mix thoroughly; bring to a bubbly boil on high heat, stirring constantly. Reduce heat to low and continue to boil mixture until a small amount of mixture forms into a soft ball when dripped in a small cup of cold water. Add margarine and vanilla. Beat by hand until glossy (about to get hard). Put pecans in just before pouring onto a large buttered dish or platter. Cut when just hard, but wait until it cools some before trying to remove from platter. Beating well is the key to this wonderful, delicious fudge. My mother made it often for our family.

## Cranberry-Orange Nut Bread

- 4 *cups unbleached flour (or you can use whole wheat for part of it)*
- 1½ *cups sugar*
- 1 *tablespoon baking powder*
- 1 *teaspoon baking soda*
- 1 *teaspoon salt*
- 2 *eggs, beaten*
- 1½ *cups orange juice*
- ½ *cup oil*
- 2 *cups cranberries, chopped*
- 1 *cup pecans or walnuts, chopped*
- 2 *teaspoons grated orange peel*

Blend dry ingredients. Beat eggs, orange juice and oil together. Add this to dry ingredients, stirring until just moist. Stir in cranberries, nuts and peel. Pour into 2 greased and floured 9x5x3-inch pans. Bake at 375° for 55 to 60 minutes. You can check with a colored wooden toothpick after 50 minutes of cooking. Always remember that oven temperatures vary. When cooled, turn out onto rack to completely cool. Wrap in Saran Wrap or foil when finished.

## Crumb Top Apple Pie

8 *large apples, peeled and sliced*
1 *cup sugar*
*Dash of nutmeg*
1 *stick of margarine or butter*
3 *tablespoons water*

Fill pie pan with apple slices, sprinkle with 1 cup sugar and nutmeg. Dot well with butter and add 3 tablespoons water.

1 *cup all-purpose flour*
1 *stick margarine or butter*
½ *cup brown sugar*
*Vanilla ice cream or whipped cream*

For upper crust, mix 1 stick butter, diced with 1 cup flour and ½ cup brown sugar. Mix well and pat over top of pie to make crust. Bake at 425° for ½ hour, then turn down to 325° and bake until brown. This is best when eaten hot with a spoonful of ice cream or whipped cream on top. A great dessert!

## Egg Nog Pound Cake

2 *sticks butter*
½ *cup shortening*
3 *cups sugar*
5 *large eggs*
1 *teaspoon vanilla*
1 *teaspoon coconut extract*
1 *teaspoon almond extract*
1 *teaspoon butternut extract*
1 *teaspoon lemon extract*
1 *teaspoon rum extract*
3 *cups cake flour*
1 *cup canned (evaporated) milk*

Cream butter, shortening and sugar. Add eggs, 1 at a time, beating well after each. Add extracts one at a time, mixing thoroughly after each addition. Alternately add flour and milk, beginning and ending with flour. Pour into a greased and floured 10-inch tube pan. Bake at 300° for 1 hour and 45 minutes.

## Fresh Coconut Candy

| | | | |
|---|---|---|---|
| 1 | *fresh coconut, grated* | ½ | *cup white corn syrup* |
| 1 | *cup brown sugar* | 1 | *tablespoon butter* |
| 1 | *cup white sugar* | ½ | *teaspoon salt* |

Grate coconut, then add all ingredients together and cook until mixture forms a soft ball when tested in cold water. Let cool. Beat until creamy, then drop by teaspoonful on waxed paper. (Another holiday necessity.)

You can make someone's day by simply sending them a note or card, or perhaps a phone call.

## Fruited Vinegar

1 *cup rice vinegar or white vinegar*

1 *individual bag raspberry, orange, blackberry or cranberry flavored tea*

In a glass container combine vinegar and tea bag. Cover and chill for 2 hours. Remove tea bag. Pour into a clean glass bottle with a lid. Use vinegar in salad dressings and in meat marinades that call for a fruit flavored vinegar. Makes 1 cup.

*This makes a perfect holiday gift. Pour vinegar into a decorative bottle, then tie a ribbon around the neck. You have a wonderful gift to share with a friend.*

# Key Lime Tarts

3 *eggs whites, room temperature*
1 *teaspoon vanilla*
1 *cup sugar*
1 *teaspoon vanilla*

**Filling**

2 *egg yolks*
1 *can condensed milk*
½ *cup lime or lemon juice*
3 *drops green food coloring*
*Whipped cream*
*Cherries (optional)*

Cover cookie sheet with waxed paper. Draw circles on paper. This recipe will make 16 small or 8 large tarts. Beat egg whites until soft peaks form. Add ⅓ cup sugar, then vanilla and remaining sugar. Mix well. Shape meringues. Take a tablespoon and indent in center of each tart. Bake at 275° for 1 hour.

While meringues are baking combine egg yolks, condensed milk, lime or lemon juice and food coloring. Mix well. When meringues are cool, place filling in center of each. Keep in refrigerator until ready to serve. Top with whipped cream and a cherry. Will keep in refrigerator for 3 to 4 days.

# Lemon Ice Box Pie

**Crust**

*1¼ cups graham cracker crumbs*
*3 tablespoons sugar*
*⅓ cup margarine, melted*

Combine graham cracker crumbs and sugar in a bowl. Stir in melted margarine and mix until thoroughly blended. Pack mixture firmly into a 9-inch pie pan and press firmly to bottom and sides, bringing crumbs up to near top. Chill one hour before filling.

**Filling**

*1 can sweetened condensed milk*
*½ cup fresh lemon juice*
*3 eggs yolks (save egg whites for meringue)*

Mix condensed milk, lemon juice and egg yolks until smooth consistency. Pour into crust.

**Meringue**

*3 egg whites (saved from filling)*
*Cream of tartar*
*¼ cup sugar*

Make meringue by whipping egg whites and cream of tartar. Gradually add sugar while beating egg whites until stiff, but not dry. Spread meringue over top of pie filling until it touches all sides. Bake in 350° oven until meringue is light brown, about 5 to 10 minutes.

## Mincemeat Cookies

- *1⅛ cups all-purpose flour*
- *¼ teaspoon baking soda*
- *½ teaspoon salt*
- *½ cup butter or margarine*
- *¼ cup brown sugar*
- *1 package crumbled mincemeat*
- *1 cup granulated sugar*
- *1 egg, beaten*
- *1 teaspoon vanilla*
- *½ cup pecans, finely chopped*

Sift flour, baking soda and salt. Cream sugar and margarine. Add egg and vanilla, blend thoroughly. Add sifted ingredients. Mix in nuts and mincemeat. Drop from teaspoon on greased cookie sheet. Bake at 350° for 10 minutes. Let cool on cookie sheet for no more than 1 minute.

*Diana Sheffield gave me this delicious recipe about 30 years ago.*

"Hanging onto resentment is letting someone you despise live rent-free in your head!"

## Mustard Sauce

- 8 *tablespoons dry mustard*
- 1 *cup sugar*
- 4 *eggs, beaten*
- ½ *cup cider vinegar*
- 1 *cup half & half*

Whip liquids together, then mix dry ingredients together. Mix both together. Cook for 1 hour over a double boiler, stirring very often. Put in clean, glass jar with cover. When cool, refrigerate. This is wonderful as a great condiment with meat, particularly pork, ham and chicken.

*Makes a great Christmas gift.*

# No-Roll Sugar Cookies

- *1 cup sugar*
- *1 cup powdered sugar*
- *1 cup margarine or butter, softened*
- *1 cup oil*
- *1 teaspoon vanilla*
- *2 eggs*
- *4¼ cups all-purpose flour*
- *1 teaspoon baking soda*
- *1 teaspoon cream of tartar*
- *1 teaspoon salt*

In large bowl beat sugars and margarine until light and fluffy. Add oil, vanilla and eggs; blend well. Stir in flour, baking soda, cream of tartar and salt; mix well. Refrigerate at least 2 hours or overnight. Heat oven to 375°. Shape dough into 1-inch balls. Roll balls in extra white sugar. Place 2 inches apart on ungreased cookie sheets. Bake for about 8 minutes (or 10 minutes for crisper cookies). Remove from cookie sheet with spatula when slightly cooled and place on wire rack until completely cool. Store in ziploc bags until ready to eat.

## Nutty Ice Box Cookies

- 1 *package pie crust mix*
- 1 *cup light brown sugar*
- 1 *egg, well beaten*
- 1 *teaspoon vanilla*
- 1 *cup pecans, chopped (or use 1 cup chocolate chips)*

Mix sugar and pie crust mix. Add well beaten egg and vanilla and mix well. Stir in nuts and shape into a roll about 10-inches long (or you can make two shorter rolls). Chill in refrigerator for several hours, then slice into ¼-inch slices. Bake on ungreased cookie sheet for 8 to 10 minutes at 375°.

*These cookies can also be frozen until a few hours before you are ready to bake. I try to keep a roll of these wonderful cookies in my freezer for when one of my grandchildren "needs" some cookies. My grandmother, Elizabeth Brown, gave me this recipe about 40 years ago, and it is still a favorite.*

## Peanut Butter Balls

2 *sticks margarine, room temperature*
1 *(16 ounce) box confectioners' sugar*
1 *cup smooth peanut butter*
1 *teaspoon vanilla*
1 *(12 ounce) package semi-sweet chocolate morsels*
*Paraffin, grated*

Combine first 4 ingredients and shape into balls. Melt chocolate morsels and a small to medium amount of grated paraffin. Dip peanut butter balls into chocolate, then set aside on aluminum foil covered trays to harden. Store in refrigerator. Delicious!

## Peanut Butter Pie

**Crust**

*1¼ cups chocolate cookie crumbs*
*¼ cup sugar*
*¼ cup butter or margarine, melted*

Combine crust ingredients then press into a 9-inch pie pan. Bake at 375° for about 8 to 10 minutes. Remove from oven and cool on rack.

**Filling**

*1 (8 ounce) package cream cheese, softened to room temperature*
*1 cup creamy peanut butter*
*1 cup sugar*
*1 tablespoon butter or margarine, softened*
*1 teaspoon vanilla*
*1 cup heavy cream, whipped*

In mixing bowl beat cream cheese, peanut butter, sugar, butter and vanilla until smooth. Fold in whipped cream. Gently spoon into crust. Garnish with grated chocolate bar, if desired.

## Pecan (or Cashew) Brittle

- 1 *cup sugar*
- ½ *cup light corn syrup*
- ⅛ *teaspoon salt*
- 2 *cups pecan halves or cashews*
- 1 *teaspoon butter*
- 1 *teaspoon vanilla extract*
- 1 *teaspoon baking soda*

In greased 2-quart glass measure, cook sugar, corn syrup, and salt on high for 2 to 3 minutes or until boiling. Cook 3 to 4 minutes. Stir in nuts, butter and vanilla. Cook 2 minutes. Immediately, stir in baking soda until light and foamy. Quickly, pour onto a greased cookie sheet or pizza pan and spread. Cool; break into pieces. Makes 1 pound.

## Pecan Pound Cake

3 *sticks margarine*
2½ *cups sugar*
8 *eggs, at room temperature*
3 *cups all-purpose flour*
1 *teaspoon almond extract*
1 *teaspoon vanilla extract*
1½ *cups chopped pecans*

Cream margarine and sugar, then add eggs and flour. Add extracts and pecans. Bake in greased and floured tube pan for 1 hour at 325°.

## Red Wine Vinegar Marinade

- 1/3 *cup red wine vinegar*
- 2 *tablespoons vegetable oil*
- 1 *tablespoon Dijon-style mustard*
- 2 *cloves garlic, minced*
- 1/4 *teaspoon dried Italian seasoning*
- 1/4 *teaspoon ground black pepper*

Combine all ingredients, stirring until well blended. Pour over meat and marinade for 15 to 30 minutes before cooking.

## Rosemary Wine Vinegar

1 *cup tightly packed fresh rosemary sprigs*
4 *tiny fresh red hot peppers*
6 *cups white wine vinegar*

Rinse rosemary sprigs, then pat dry with paper towels. In a stainless steel or glass saucepan combine the rosemary sprigs, hot peppers and vinegar. Crush rosemary lightly with the back of a spoon. Bring mixture to near boiling. Remove from heat and cool. Pour mixture into a clean 2-quart jar. Cover the jar tightly with a nonmetal lid (or cover the jar with plastic wrap, then tightly seal with a metal lid). Let stand in a cool, dark place for 2 weeks before using.

# Rosemary's Secret Crumb Cake

3 *cups all-purpose flour*
1 *tablespoon baking powder*
2 *cups sugar*
1 *teaspoon salt*
½ *cup melted butter*

Mix until crumbly. Take out 1 cup of mixture for topping and set aside.

1 *egg*
*Milk*

Beat 1 egg in measuring cup and fill to 1 cup with milk. Add to mixture in bowl above. Mix well. Put in greased 8-inch square cake pan.

2 *teaspoons cinnamon*
2 *tablespoons sugar*

Add the cinnamon and sugar to the cup of crumbs and spread on top of dough. Bake at 350° for about 50 minutes or until toothpick tester comes out clean.

*I have added raisins to this cake. I have also put strawberry jam on top about 15 minutes before done. This is a heavy coffee cake of German origin.*

## Shortbread Cookies

*2 cups all-purpose flour*
*1 cup butter*
*½ teaspoon baking powder*
*½ cup sugar*
*1 egg, unbeaten*
*Grated rind of 1 lemon*

Sift flour and baking powder together. Using table or hand mixer, cream butter thoroughly, slowly adding sugar, beating until smooth. Stir in unbeaten egg and lemon rind. Add dry ingredients to mixture, then pour onto lightly floured board and work (mix with your clean hands) together until smooth. Divide dough into 2 parts and place each half on greased 9-inch pie plate. Flatten with your fingers and press into shape on bottom of pans. Mark into pie shaped wedges with the back of a knife (or you can just press into a greased 8x8-inch pan and prick with a fork). Bake in slow oven (300°) for 30 minutes, or 45 minutes to get crunchier. This dough will make 16 servings or may be cut into fancy shapes with cookie cutters.

## Sour Cream Pound Cake

*1 cup margarine, softened*
*2¾ cups sugar*
*6 eggs, at room temperature*
*3 cups sifted all-purpose flour*
*½ teaspoon salt*
*¼ teaspoon baking soda*
*1 (8 ounce) carton sour cream*
*1 teaspoon vanilla flavoring*
*½ teaspoon almond flavoring*

Cream margarine and sugar until light. Add eggs, one at a time, beating thoroughly after each. Sift dry ingredients and add alternately with sour cream to butter and sugar mixture, beating until smooth. Always begin and end with your flour mixture. Add flavorings. Pour into a 9-inch tube pan sprayed with nonstick vegetable spray. Bake in 350° oven for 1 hour and 20 minutes or until done. Let stand in pan on rack about 10 to 15 minutes. Turn onto cooling rack. Can be eaten as is or topped with your favorite frosting. (My favorite is Penuche).

## Easy Penuche Icing

*1 cup butter or margarine*
*2 cups light brown sugar, packed*
*½ cup milk*
*4 cups sifted confectioners' sugar*

Melt butter in saucepan. Add brown sugar and boil over low heat for 2 to 3 minutes, stirring constantly. Stir in milk. Bring to a boil, stirring constantly. Remove from heat and cool to lukewarm. Gradually add confectioners' sugar. Beat until thick enough to spread. If icing becomes too stiff, add a little hot water. Spread over cake. Top of cake can be decorated easily with pecan halves or chopped pecans.

# Southern Pecan Cheesecake

**Crust**

*1½ cups quick oats*
*1 cup pecans, finely chopped*
*½ cup brown sugar*
*⅓ cup margarine, melted*

To make crust, place oats in food blender and process to consistency of flour. Combine oats with remaining crust ingredients then press into bottom of a 10-inch spring form pan. Chill.

**Filling**

*5 (8 ounce) packages cream cheese*
*1⅔ cups light brown sugar*
*5 eggs*
*1 teaspoon vanilla*
*2 cups pecans, chopped and divided*

Beat cream cheese in mixer until fluffy, slowly adding brown sugar and mix well. Add eggs, one at a time, mixing after each addition. Stir in vanilla and ½ of nuts. Mix and pour over crust. Bake at 350° for 1 hour. Turn oven off, but leave cake in oven for 30 minutes more. To reduce chance of cracks on top surface run knife around edge of cheesecake as soon as you remove it from oven. Let cool to room temperature. Chill for 8 hours. Remove sides of pan. Press remaining chopped pecans around sides and top with whipped cream, if desired.

## Toffee Bars

*1 cup sugar*
*1 cup butter*
*¼ cup water*
*½ cup semi-sweet chocolate chips*
*½ cup finely chopped pecans or sliced almonds*

Heat sugar, butter and water to boiling in a 2-quart saucepan, stirring constantly; reduce to medium heat. Cook, stirring constantly to 300° on candy thermometer or until a small amount of mixture dropped into a cup of very cold water separates into hard, brittle threads. Be careful mixture doesn't burn.

Immediately pour toffee onto ungreased cookie sheet. Quickly spread to ¼-inch thick. Sprinkle with chocolate chips; let stand about 1 minute until soft. Sprinkle with nuts. Let stand until firm. Twist cookie sheet to break the toffee loose. Break into pieces. Store in covered container in refrigerator.

*This is wonderful candy!*

## Walnut Pie

3 *egg whites, beaten stiff*
½ *teaspoon baking powder*
1 *cup sugar*
1 *cup walnuts, chopped*
18 *crumbled saltines*
1 *teaspoon vanilla*
½ *pint whipping cream*
2 *tablespoons sugar*

Beat egg whites until stiff, then add sugar and baking powder. Fold in saltines, walnuts and vanilla. Pour into well-buttered 9-inch pie plate and bake at 325° for 25 minutes. Cool. Beat whipping cream, gradually adding 2 tablespoons sugar, then pour over pie. Spread whipping cream to edges of crust. Whipping cream must be added at least 4 to 5 hours before serving. Refrigerate. Garnish with cherries before serving.

*Give this pie a try. You will love it!*

## Devils Food Cookies

*3¼ cups flour*
*½ cup baking cocoa*
*½ teaspoon salt*
*½ teaspoon baking soda*
*1 cup (2 sticks) butter, room temperature*
*1½ cups sugar*
*2 eggs, room temperature*
*1 teaspoon vanilla*
*1 cup chocolate chips*
*Assorted frostings and decorations*

Sift together flour, cocoa, salt and baking soda into medium bowl. Set aside. Beat together butter and sugar until fluffy in large bowl using electric mixer at medium to high speed. At medium speed beat in the eggs, one at a time, then add vanilla. Stir in chocolate chips. Slowly add the flour mixture. It will make a stiff dough. Cover bowl with foil or plastic wrap and refrigerate for at least 3 hours. Preheat oven to 350°.

Roll out ¼ of dough at a time on a floured surface. Roll to about ¼-inch thick. Cut into assorted shapes using cookie cutters. Place on a cookie sheet and bake in 350° oven for about 10 minutes or until firm. Remove to wire rack with thin spatula and let cool.

*Decorate with frosting and/or sprinkles, nuts, raisins, cherries, etc. Be creative!*

## Roasted Pecans

*1 pound (16 ounces) pecan halves*
*1 stick butter, melted*
*Salt*

Place pecan halves on a large cookie sheet and bake in 250° oven for 25 to 30 minutes. About 5 minutes before done, remove pan from oven and pour butter over pecans, then lightly sprinkle with salt. Stir, then return to oven for the remaining 5 minutes.

*Roasted pecans were always as much a part of our Christmas meals as the turkey and dressing. However, they are delicious as part of your appetizers. Always try to serve in your prettiest little dish.*

# Notes

# Vegetarian Christmas

# Granddaughters

My oldest granddaughter, Elizabeth,
is a vegetarian and this section is dedicated to her with love.
All of us who cook in our family have had to learn to leave the meat out of Elizabeth's food. No seasoning with meat, no broths, no nothing. Not an easy thing to always remember when you are cooking for a large group of "meat eaters", but it can be done. And, as the years have gone by it has gotten easier and easier.

I realize there are many degrees of vegetarian eating, but the only one I am personally knowledgeable about is the way my granddaughter Elizabeth eats - no meats.

I hope these recipes will be appealing to your vegetarian, or perhaps to your whole family. Enjoy!

## Baked Asparagus

- 1 *can cream of mushroom soup, undiluted*
- 1 *teaspoon prepared mustard*
- 4 *hard-boiled eggs, sliced*
- 1 *(1 pound) can asparagus spears, drained*

Preheat oven to 425°. Combine soup and mustard. In a 1-quart casserole alternate layers of eggs, asparagus and soup. Bake 15 to 20 minutes or until hot.

It is just as important to forget a wrong
as it is to remember a kindness.

## Baked Spinach

- *1 package frozen spinach, thawed*
- *1 egg, beaten*
- *1 cup sharp Cheddar cheese, grated*
- *½ can mushroom soup*
- *½ cup onion, finely chopped*
- *½ cup mayonnaise (not diet)*
- *1 cup bread crumbs*

Mix together well. Place in casserole dish and cover with toasted, buttered bread crumbs. Bake at 350° for 25 to 30 minutes. Serve hot.

*Most spinach haters love this dish!*

For God so loved the world, that he gave his only begotten Son…"
(John 3:16)

# Banana Split Cake

*2 cups graham cracker crumbs*
*1 stick butter or margarine, softened*
*1 box confectioners' sugar*
*1 (8 ounce) cream cheese, softened*
*1 egg (or egg substitute)*
*4-6 bananas*
*1 large can crushed pineapple, drained*
*1 large Cool Whip (can be fat free), room temperature*
*Few chopped nuts (pecans or walnuts)*
*Cherries for decoration*

Mix graham cracker crumbs with margarine and press into 8x11-inch glass dish. Combine confectioners' sugar, cream cheese and egg. Beat together until smooth. Pour over graham cracker crumbs. Slice bananas over mixture. Pour crushed pineapple over bananas. Spread Cool Whip over pineapple. Sprinkle nuts over top. Add cherries now, or just before serving. Place in refrigerator until ready to cut and serve.

*This no-cook dessert serves 12 to 16 and is even better if prepared a day ahead. The tart pineapple keeps the bananas "happy".*

## Broccoli Casserole

*1 package chopped broccoli*
*1 can cream of mushroom soup*
*½ cup sharp Cheddar cheese, grated*
*1 egg*
*½ cup mayonnaise*
*1 tablespoon onion, grated*
*Salt and pepper to taste*
*½ cup buttered bread crumbs*

Cook chopped broccoli for 5 minutes in small amount of water in saucepan, or for about 3 minutes in microwave, drain. Mix remaining ingredients, except bread crumbs, and add to broccoli. Pour into a greased baking dish and top with buttered bread crumbs. Bake in 400° oven for 20 minutes.

"Count your blessings;
name them one by one."
(Proverbs 37:8 TLB)

# Broccoli Rice Casserole

- 1 *small onion, finely chopped*
- ½ *cup celery, finely chopped*
- 1 *(10 ounce) package frozen broccoli, thawed and chopped*
- 1 *tablespoon butter*
- 1 *(8 ounce) jar processed cheese spread*
- 1 *can cream of mushroom soup, undiluted*
- 1 *(5 ounce) can evaporated milk*
- 3 *cups cooked rice*

Sauté onion, celery and broccoli in butter in a large skillet for about 5 minutes. Stir cheese, soup and milk into broccoli mixture and stir until smooth. Place rice in a greased 8-inch square baking dish, then pour cheese mixture over rice but do not stir. Bake uncovered at 325° for about 30 minutes.

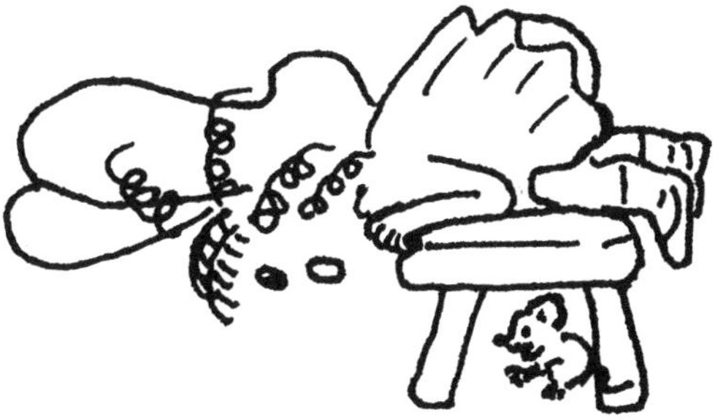

## Chocolate Pecan Clusters

*1 (7 ounce) jar marshmallow cream*
*1½ pounds candy kisses*
*5 cups sugar*
*1 (12 ounce) can evaporated milk*
*½ cup butter or margarine*
*6 cups pecan halves*

Place marshmallow cream and chocolate kisses in a large bowl. Bring sugar, milk and butter to a boil in heavy saucepan, stirring constantly for approximately 8 minutes. Pour over marshmallow cream and chocolate kisses and stir until well mixed and chocolate kisses are melted. Mix pecans in chocolate mixture. Drop by rounded teaspoons onto a waxed paper lined baking sheet. Chill until firm. Store in refrigerator in closed container. Makes approximately 12 dozen.

## Frosted Cauliflower

- 1 *large head cauliflower*
- ½ *cup mayonnaise*
- 2 *teaspoons prepared mustard*
- 1 *cup (4 ounces) grated Cheddar cheese*
- *Paprika*
- *Tomato wedges (optional)*

Wash cauliflower; remove leaves and cut out core. Cook, covered, in boiling, salted water for 12 to 15 minutes or until tender; drain. Place cauliflower in a shallow ungreased baking pan. Combine mayonnaise and mustard; spread over cauliflower. Bake at 375° for 5 minutes. Top with cheese and bake an additional 4 minutes. Sprinkle lightly with paprika and garnish with tomato wedges if desired. Good!

## Frozen Cranberry Salad

*1 (16 ounce) can whole berry cranberry sauce*
*1 (8¼ ounce) can crushed pineapple, drained*
*1 (8 ounce) carton sour cream*
*½ cup chopped pecans*

Combine ingredients and mix well. Spoon mixture into paper-lined muffin tins. Freeze several hours or until firm. Remove from muffin tins, place in zip lock bags, seal and return to freezer until 10 minutes before ready to serve.

Children and grandchildren will not remember you for the material things you buy for them, but for the feeling that you always loved them...no matter what. I do not remember my grandfather ever telling me that he loved me, but I always knew. He always smiled at me and made me feel very special, and he held me on his lap and told me wonderful stories. He always made time to answer all my questions. He was the best!

## Green Bean Casserole

- 1 *medium onion, chopped*
- 2 *tablespoons butter or margarine*
- 1 *small jar mushrooms, sliced*
- 1 *can cream of mushroom soup*
- 2 *cans cut green beans, drained*
- 1 *cup sharp Cheddar cheese, shredded*
- 1 *can French fried onion rings*

Sauté onion in margarine in large frying pan. Add mushroom pieces, green beans and cheese. Mix gently until cheese melts. Place in a casserole and top with the onion rings. Heat in 350° oven for 25 to 30 minutes. Serve hot.

## Marinated Vegetables

- 1 *cup cucumbers, thinly sliced*
- 1 *cup yellow squash, thinly sliced*
- 1 *cup carrots, thinly sliced*
- 1 *medium onion, thinly sliced and separated*
- 1 *cup vinegar*
- ¾ *cup sugar*
- ¼ *cup salad oil*
- 1 *teaspoon salt*
- ¼ *teaspoon pepper*

Combine vegetables in large container. Combine other ingredients in jar and shake. Pour over vegetables. Cover bowl and refrigerate overnight or several hours. Keeps well in refrigerator for several days.

## Mashed Potato Cakes

*1 cup mashed potatoes*
*1 egg*
*Salt and pepper to taste*
*1 tablespoon grated sharp Cheddar cheese*
*1 teaspoon onion, finely grated*
*Flour*

Mix potatoes and slightly beaten egg together; add salt and pepper. Add cheese and onion; shape into rounded flat cakes about ½-inch thick. Coat lightly with flour. Heat cooking oil in large, heavy skillet. Fry potato cakes on medium heat. Brown on both sides. Serve warm.

*When I was growing up all leftover mashed potatoes went into potato cakes. We loved them!*

# Ratatouille

*1 medium eggplant*
*4 medium ripe tomatoes*
*⅓ cup olive oil*
*2 cloves garlic, pressed*
*2 teaspoons parsley, minced*
*¼ teaspoon freshly ground pepper*
*1 large red bell pepper, cubed*
*3 small zucchini*
*2 medium onions, finely chopped*
*1½ teaspoons salt*
*1 teaspoon sugar*

Trim the stem from the eggplant, but do not peel. Cut into ½-inch slices, then cut into cubes. Place the eggplant cubes in a bowl with salted water to cover. Weight the eggplant down with a plate. Let it soak for at least 15 minutes. Remove the seeds and membranes from the red bell pepper, then cut into strips and chop coarsely. Peel the tomatoes and chop coarsely. Cut ends from the zucchini, then slice crosswise thinly. Heat oil in a Dutch oven until sizzling, then add onions, sweet bell pepper and zucchini. Cover and cook for 5 minutes, stirring occasionally. Combine the garlic and parsley, then stir into the onion mixture. Drain the eggplant thoroughly, then add eggplant to mixture. Cover and cook 5 minutes. Add tomatoes, salt, pepper and sugar, mixing thoroughly. Cover and cook 10 to 15 minutes longer until flavors blend and eggplant is tender. Serve hot.

*The Ratatouille can be cooked in your microwave after the onions, pepper and zucchini has been browned in Dutch oven.*

# Squash and Tomato Casserole

2 *pounds small yellow squash, sliced*
2 *medium zucchini squash, sliced*
2 *medium or 1 large onion, finely chopped*
1 *cup water (approximately)*
2 *large ripe tomatoes*
*Salt and pepper to taste*
1 *cup (4 ounces) grated sharp Cheddar cheese*
½ *cup (2 ounces) grated hot pepper cheese*

Combine squash and onions in water. Cover. Bring to a boil, then turn to low heat. Cook until squash is soft. Drain off water. Cut out stem area from tomatoes and make an X slash on bottom of each. Place in boiling water to cover for about 30 to 45 seconds. Remove from water at once; skins remove easily from tomato. Cut tomato into small pieces and add to squash. Add salt and pepper to taste. Add cheeses and stir well. Pour into baking dish and bake in 350° oven for 30 minutes. Serve while hot. Yum! Serves 6.

## Stuffed Celery

*Celery stalks*
*½ cup pecans, finely cut*
*2 tablespoons milk*
*8 ounces cream cheese, softened to room temperature*

Clean celery. Combine pecans, milk and cream cheese and mix well. Stuff mixture into celery stalk pieces. Refrigerate until ready to use.

*Celery stuffed with pimento cheese is also delicious!*

"Tell someone you love
that you love them; tell them again."
(Romans 5:5)

## Swiss Cheese and Mushroom Pie

*1 teaspoon butter*
*1½ cups chopped onion*
*½ pound mushrooms, sliced*
*½ teaspoon salt*
*Black pepper, to taste*
*Pinch of thyme*
*½ teaspoon dry mustard*
*4 large eggs*
*1½ cups milk*
*2 tablespoons flour*
*1½ cups grated Swiss cheese, packed*
*Paprika*
*Fresh tomato slices*
*Unbaked pie crust*

Preheat oven to 375°. Melt butter in a medium frying pan. Add onions and sauté over medium heat for 5 minutes. When they begin to soften, add mushrooms, salt, pepper, thyme and mustard. Sauté about 5 minutes more then remove from heat. Combine eggs, milk and flour in a blender or food processor and beat well. Spread cheese over the bottom of the unbaked pie crust and spread the onion-mustard mixture on top. Pour in the egg-milk mixture and sprinkle the top with paprika. Arrange fresh tomato slices on top. Bake for 35 to 45 minutes or until solid in the center. Insert a table knife part way in the center. If it comes out clean the pie is done. Serve warm.

## Vanilla Ice Cream

*4 eggs, beaten*
*¾ cup sugar*
*1 large can evaporated milk*
*½ pint whipping cream*
*1 can condensed milk*

Mix above ingredients well and place in ice cream maker. Add whole milk to fill line of ice cream maker. Add ice and churn according to ice cream freezer directions.

*Chopped fruits such as peaches, bananas, etc. can be added before pouring into ice cream maker. You can also add "oreo" cookies broken into pieces. Add this about half way through ice cream machine mixing time.*

## Vegetable Casserole

*1 can French style green beans*
*1 can shoepeg corn*
*½ cup celery, diced*
*½ cup green pepper, diced*
*½ cup onion, diced*
*½ cup sour cream*
*1 can cream of celery soup*
*Salt and pepper to taste*

Mix together and refrigerate overnight.

*½ cup cracker crumbs*
*½ cup butter, melted*

Sprinkle crumbs over mix and drizzle with butter. Bake at 350° for 45 minutes.

# Christmas Gift

Christmas is typically considered a season of generosity. Most people relish the giving and receiving of gifts, myself included. However, there is one gift that people in my family continuously try to give away on Christmas morning that I will do everything possible to refuse and any dirty trick I can to give it to them instead. That loathed item? None other than a "Christmas Gift".

Didn't I just say that I love getting gifts? Well, there is an exception to the rule. For 5 generations, my family has tried to unload the burden of the title of the Christmas Gift loser to one side or another. Much to my chagrin, my house has lost two years in a row now. Each Christmas morning, when all of the houses have opened their gifts, (the competitors include the senior Browning's house, my grandparents, where the Masts traditionally are and the Guth/Browning and Hunter houses) the game begins. Some brave body will call the Browning household to try to say "Christmas Gift" first, or if you're lucky, a representative for the Browning family will try to call you.

Now, I cannot give away all of my secrets to winning this highly competitive game - remember that there is only one chance to win or lose, and the results last an entire year - but I will indulge you with a few.

First, don't let younger brothers call the Browning house. They mean well, but don't understand the importance of the game yet. Secondly, let the other household call you. Think about it: if you call them, they have the advantage of being the one to pick up the phone and yell the phrase first. It is difficult to be sure when the phone has been picked up when you are calling. You have to be on your toes if you call. So kids, don't try that at home. Step out of the line here if you have any heart conditions, are pregnant or have any other serious conditions. Calling the family is not for the faint of heart.

Christmas is a season of love and giving, but for that brief phone call early Christmas morning, I throw all that out the window. Although highly competitive and perhaps a bit unappealing to some, this nail-biting moment is one of the most enjoyable memories for me at Christmas. However, after being away at college for two years now, being able to see my family just may begin outranking that phone call.

*Elizabeth Guth (Jeannine's granddaughter)*

# Hansel and Gretel's House

# Christmas In Our Town

Christmas in our town,
Was a wonderful time of year.
The memories are warm and happy.
Each precious day I hold dear.

Santa came to our church,
Each and every year.
To pass out gifts to every child,
Who came from far and near.

The Christmas tree was tall and stately,
The best that could be found.
No one ever bought a Christmas tree,
They just claimed a special one that grew in our town.

When Christmas Eve arrived,
We sang carols all around town.
Each family made cookies and candy,
There was always enough to go around.

Sleep was hard to come by,
Each Christmas Eve at night.
But we knew Santa would come by our house,
So that made everything all right.

Christmas morning was so happy!
We opened our stockings with care.
Then we drove one mile to our grandparent's home,
And ripped open our gifts as fast as we would dare.

A special part of Christmas,
Was all the delicious food we ate.
We started early with roasted pecans,
Which we snitched from a cut glass plate.

The green olives were wonderful, too,
Even though they were an acquired taste.
The turkey, dressing and gravy were always best,
As we gulped them down in thankful haste.

Christmas in our town,
Filled my life with joy and love.
I couldn't dream of a happier childhood,
And, for all those precious memories, I thank my
Father above.

Jeannine Browning

# Hansel and Gretel Cottage

*1 cup vegetable shortening*
*1 cup packed brown sugar*
*1 cup molasses*
*2 eggs*
*2½ teaspoons cinnamon*
*2 teaspoons ground ginger*
*1 teaspoon ground allspice*
*½ teaspoon ground cloves*
*¼ teaspoon salt*
*6 cups all-purpose flour*
*2 tablespoons baking powder*
*2 recipes Gingerbread House and Cookie Icing (see page 110)*
*Assorted candies*

In a large bowl, beat together shortening, brown sugar, molasses and eggs until thoroughly blended. Beat in cinnamon, ginger, allspice, cloves and salt. Add flour and baking powder, beating until well blended. Dough will be sticky. Divide dough into 2 equal portions. Wrap each portion in a plastic bag; refrigerate 1 hour or longer. To bake gingerbread, preheat oven to 300°. Line 2 (18x2-inch) sheet cake pans with heavy-duty aluminum foil; grease foil. You may use one pan twice. Using a rolling pin, roll each portion of dough out on one greased, foil-lined pan in an even layer, filling pan completely. Place 2 side and 2 roof patterns on one pan. Place front and back house patterns on other pan. Cut around them carefully, do not separate or remove dough from pan. Cut out door and heart-shaped or square windows. Cut extra space on side with a small cookie cutter making trees, gingerbread boys and girls, but do not remove from pan. Use these cookies as decorations around the yard of the house. Bake pans of dough, one at a time, in center of oven 55 to 65 minutes. Watch carefully to avoid overbrowning. Longer baking time is necessary for a harder cookie - important for a sturdy house. Remove pan from oven; immediately re-cut dough pieces, removing any excess gingerbread. Remove small dough pieces, including cookies, and place on rack to cool. Let large house pieces cool in pan, loosening carefully underneath with spatula while still warm. Allow house pieces to dry overnight before assembling.

*For a darker house, add ¼ cup cocoa powder. For a lighter color house, use 1 cup Karo syrup instead of molasses.*

**Gingerbread House and Cookie Icing**

- 4 *egg whites*
- 1 *(1 pound) package powdered sugar (3¾ cups)*
- ¼ *teaspoon cream of tartar*

In a medium bowl, beat together egg whites, powdered sugar and cream of tartar with electric mixer at low speed until blended. Turn mixer to high speed; continue beating 7 to 10 minutes until thick and soft peaks form and a knife drawn through mixture leaves a clean cut path. Use immediately or cover and store in airtight container in refrigerator. Use within 1 to 2 days. Once you begin working with the icing, keep it covered with a damp towel to prevent drying out. This icing dries hard. Makes about 3¾ cups icing. You may want to use food coloring to tint some of the icing for cookie trees or people.

*Remember to make 2 batches of icing for House and Cookies. Use as cement when building cookie houses or to frost or decorate cookies.*

**Assembling Gingerbread House**

Using a round 16 to 18-inch diameter piece of Styrofoam or cardboard as a base, draw lines at a right angle on the base where you want the front and left side wall of house to stand. Keep the icing covered with a damp towel during assembly or it will dry out. Place icing in a large pastry bag fitted with a large plain round ¼ to ½-inch diameter decorating tube, filling half- full at a time. Ice over the lines on base of house with tube icing. Place side wall upright in place, then pipe a strip of icing up edges where front wall will be attached. Stand front wall in place, attaching to side wall at right angle. Hold the pieces upright for a few minutes until icing has set. Then prop walls up placing a heavy jar in corner for support. Let stand 30 minutes or longer until icing sets. Remove jar. With icing, cement right side wall of house to front, piping icing strip on base and on edge of front wall as before. Put icing on base and on side walls where back will attach. Put back piece in place. Let stand 30 minutes or until set. Ice top edges of house; lay roof pieces over them, using jar or can under roof overhangs to prevent slippage while drying. Roof pieces should meet but not overlap. Fill any space between them with icing. Make sure all seams of house are filled with icing, then let stand until all icing has dried. Frost roof and decorate with assorted candies. Use large pastry bag fitted with small round decorating tube. Decorate sides, front and back of house with windows, shutters, flowers and designs. Icing can be tinted. Add candy pieces. Spread icing and completely cover yard or base of house and decorate. Add door to house by applying icing strip to door opening and standing door in place. Decorate cookie shapes, and place in yard using icing. Assorted candies to decorate the house should be on hand in good supply when icing the roof and sides of the house. A wide variety of candies spark the imagination. You can frost a cardboard cut out to place gingerbread house on for foundation with stand up trees, snowmen, angels, etc. Have fun and use your imagination. Children can help.

*Diagram on next page*

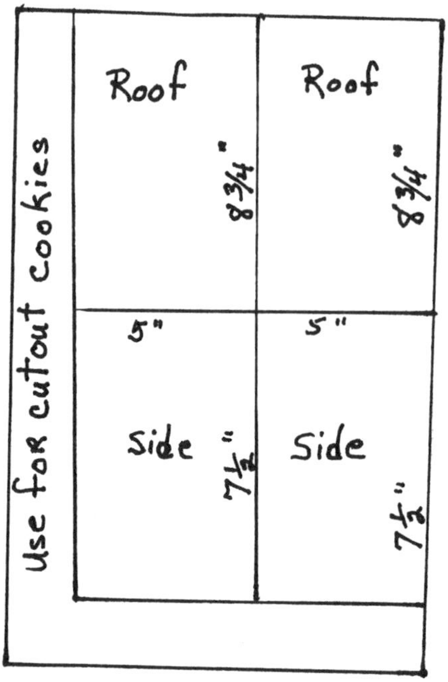
Roof
Roof
8 3/4"
8 3/4"
Use for cutout cookies
5"
5"
Side
Side
7 1/2"
7 1/2"

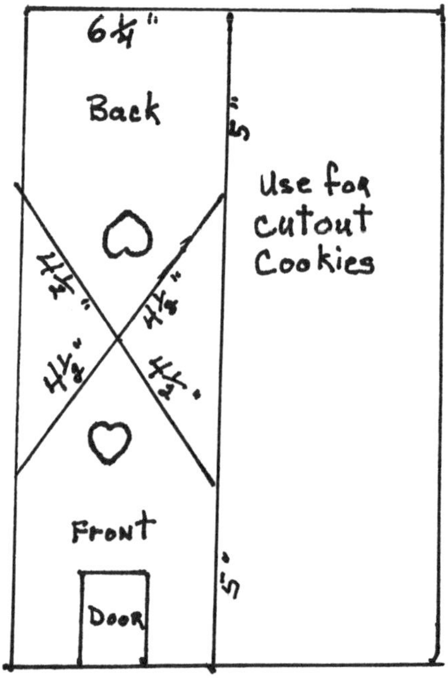
6 1/4"
Back
5"
Use for cutout Cookies
4 1/2"
4 1/2"
4 1/2"
4 1/2"
Front
5"
Door

# Happy Birthday Jesus

# Happy Birthday Jesus Party

Send out simple invitations made by you or your children, or telephone everyone. Since our family is so large we usually just include our family, but inviting others is also great!

We order a large sheet cake from our favorite bakery for this event because I am usually too busy to bake another cake. This year I took in a Christmas card with a picture of Jesus, Mary and Joseph and a small group of children and the cake shop made a picture of the card and put it on the cake. We also had Happy Birthday Jesus on the cake, and all the names of our grandchildren.

We placed the cake on the dining room table with candles on it, had our ceremony, sang "Happy Birthday, Jesus", then lit the candles. All the grandchildren took turns blowing out the candles. Then, we cut the cake and ate it! What a special memory!

Let one of your children or grandchildren read the Christmas story from the Bible.

Another child can tell the Christmas story, etc.

Begin a memory for your children/grandchildren that they will continue when they are grown. Keep Jesus in Christmas!

When you were small and I held you in my arms,
I wrapped you in soft blankets and held you tight.
Now that you are grown and on your own,
I fold my hands and cover you with prayers.

## Cheese Log or Ball

- *1 container Kaukauna sharp Cheddar cheese*
- *1 container Kaukauna Swiss Almond cheese*
- *1 (8 ounce) package cream cheese*
- *1-2 cups pecans, chopped*

Mix the 3 cheeses together until smooth. Easy to mix if all are at room temperature. Shape into 2 logs or balls and roll in chopped pecans. Serve with assorted crackers.

"Make a joyful noise unto the Lord."
(Psalm 66:1-2)

## Fancy Ham Sandwiches

2 *sticks margarine, melted*
2 *tablespoons poppy seed*
2 *small onions, finely chopped*
5 *tablespoons mustard (regular)*
½-1 *pound Swiss cheese, sliced thin*
½-1 *pound ham, sliced thin*
3 *packages small dinner rolls (bakery rolls, if possible)*

Mix first 4 ingredients and let stand until spreadable. Slice rolls in half and spread mixture on both halves. Layer cheese and ham - cut or folded to fit roll. Place on baking sheet and bake at 325° until cheese is melted. Serve warm.

*Leftovers can be placed in covered container and refrigerated. Reheat when ready to use.*

# Fruit Punch

- 1 *(12 ounce) can frozen orange juice concentrate*
- 1 *(12 ounce) can frozen lemonade concentrate*
- 1 *(46 ounce) can unsweetened pineapple juice*
- 1 *quart apricot juice*
- 2 *cups unsweetened grapefruit juice*
- ¾ *cup sugar*
- 1 *large bottle ginger ale, chilled*
- *Orange slices or cherries*

Combine juices and sugar in a covered container and stir well. Chill. To serve, add ginger ale. Garnish with orange slices or cherries.

## Holiday Cranberry Punch

2 *cups orange juice*
½ *cup lemon juice*
½ *cup sugar*
1 *(48 ounce) bottle cranberry juice cocktail*
2 *pints raspberry sherbet*
2 *(46 ounce) bottles ginger ale, chilled*

Combine orange juice, lemon juice and sugar; stir until sugar dissolves. Add cranberry juice; mix well. Chill. Spoon scoops of sherbet on top of punch. Add ginger ale; gently stir to blend. Makes 3½ quarts.

"Count your blessings;
name them one by one."
(Proverbs 10:22)

## Hot Cranberry Punch

- *1 (48 ounce) bottle cranberry juice cocktail*
- *1 cup water*
- *½ cup firmly packed brown sugar*
- *¾ teaspoon ground cloves*
- *½ teaspoon ground allspice*
- *½ teaspoon ground cinnamon*
- *¼ teaspoon ground nutmeg*
- *1 (46 ounce) can pineapple juice*

Combine all ingredients except pineapple juice in a large saucepan; mix well. Bring to a boil, stirring occasionally. Add pineapple juice; return to boil. Reduce heat and simmer about 5 minutes. Serve hot. Makes about 3 quarts.

## Pineapple-Orange Punch

- *½ gallon orange sherbet*
- *1 (46 ounce) can pineapple juice, chilled*
- *1 (33.8 ounce) bottle ginger ale, chilled*
- *3 cups orange drink, chilled*
- *3 cups lemon lime carbonated drink, chilled*

Place sherbet in a large punch bowl; add remaining ingredients and stir well. Makes 5 quarts.

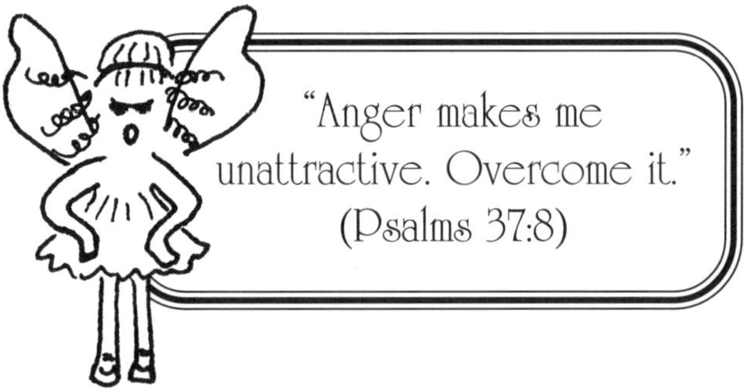

"Anger makes me unattractive. Overcome it."
(Psalms 37:8)

## Bea's Best Punch

- 3 *(3 ounce) packages raspberry jello*
- 13 *cups water, divided*
- 4 *cups sugar*
- 1 *(16 ounce) bottle lemon concentrate*
- 1 *ounce almond extract*
- 2 *(46 ounce) cans pineapple juice*
- 4 *quarts ginger ale*

Dissolve jello in 4 cups boiling water. Add sugar, lemon juice, almond extract, 9 cups water and pineapple juice. Seal in a plastic storage container and freeze. Do not fill completely to the top. Take out of freezer 3 hours before serving. Add ginger ale just before serving. (This should be made up and frozen at least 2 to 3 days before using.)

*This makes a wonderful, slushy juice punch which is popular with all ages!*

## Orange-Coconut Pound Cake

*1½ cups butter, softened*
*2 cups sugar*
*8 eggs, room temperature*
*Grated rind of 2 oranges*
*4 cups all-purpose flour*
*3 teaspoons baking powder*
*1¼ cups grated coconut, divided*
*1¼ cups orange juice*

Cream butter with sugar until light and fluffy. Beat in eggs, one at a time. Stir in orange rind. Toss together flour, baking powder and ½ cup coconut. Add to butter mixture alternately with orange juice, stirring until smooth.

Pour into a greased and floured 10-inch tube pan or Bundt pan. Bake in preheated 350° oven about 1¼ hours or until cake tests done with a colored wooden toothpick. Cool 15 minutes on a cake rack. When warm remove to serving plate and pour glaze over cake, letting it run down the sides. Sprinkle top with remaining ¾ cup coconut.

**Orange Glaze**

*1½ cups confectioners' sugar*
*1 tablespoon orange rind*
*3 tablespoons orange juice*

Combine sugar, orange rind and orange juice; beat until smooth.

# Scripture Cake

**Apple Raisin Cake**

- 2½ *cups all-purpose flour (II Samuel 13:8)*
- 5 *teaspoons baking powder (Galatians 5:8)*
- ½ *teaspoon salt (Mark 9:50)*
- ¾ *teaspoon cinnamon (I Kings 10:10)*
- 3 *tablespoons butter (Proverbs 30:33)*
- ¾ *cup sugar (Jeremiah 6:20)*
- 1 *egg (Isaiah 10:14)*
- ¾ *cup milk (I Corinthians 3:2)*
- 1½ *cups apple, peeled and sliced (Proverbs 25:11)*
- ½ *cup raisins (I Samuel 30:12)*

Preheat oven to 350°. Sift dry ingredients together. Cream butter and sugar. Add egg to butter mixture and mix. Add dry ingredients alternately with milk. Mix in apple and raisins by hand. Pour into a greased loaf pan. Bake approximately 90 minutes.

## Christmas Memories

I close my eyes and think of Christmas past and present with all the pungent smells of cut trees fresh from the woods and the oven aromas of golden brown turkey, pumpkin and apple pies my mother and grandmother caringly prepared. Now I, in my turn, have taken on the mantel of tender of the feast. I remember the long transition from one generation to the other so slowly it seemed then, and how we took our place from watching and learning to the teacher of our children and grandchildren. All our loved ones gathered around us, if not in mortal flesh, then in memory, hold close what is dearest to our hearts and most meaningful to who we are and what we become is centered in the family, the traditions we pass down and the true meaning of our life.

Christmas is that special time and may we celebrate it into eternity.

*Rosemary Fry (Ossenfort) Brofos*
2001 *A.D.*

*Christmas Caroling is a wonderful experience. Just practice a few Christmas hymns with your family and friends and go up and down your street to serenade your friends. Be brave, ring doorbells and sing two or three songs, then be on your way to the next house.*

*Some suggestions are "Silent Night", "Away in a Manger", and ending with "We Wish You a Merry Christmas and a Happy New Year". You will have a great time. Return to your home for punch, cookies, etc. Christmas Caroling can be done on Christmas Eve or whenever you can get your group together...even several days before Christmas or Christmas night. Have fun!*

# Christmas Eve

# Christmas Eve

Christmas Eve is a special time when families gather together to celebrate the birth of Jesus. Many will be attending early church services, then returning home for a special meal together. Hopefully some of these recipes will be perfect for your family. Many can be prepared in advance, then cooked or warmed when ready to eat. Enjoy!

# Christmas Eve

Christmas Eve is a special time when families gather together to celebrate the birth of Jesus. Many will be attending early church services, then returning home for a special meal together. Hopefully some of these recipes will be perfect for your family. Many can be prepared in advance, then cooked or warmed when ready to eat. Enjoy!

## Artichoke Dip

*1 can artichokes, drained and crumbled*
*¾ cup mayonnaise*
*1 cup Parmesan cheese*
*Paprika*

Combine artichokes, mayonnaise and cheese. Place in 1-quart baking dish. Sprinkle paprika on top. Bake at 350° for 20 minutes, uncovered. Serve hot with crackers.

*In microwave, decrease mayonnaise to ½ cup and bake on high for about 5 minutes, stirring after 2½ minutes. Sprinkle with paprika after taking from microwave.*

## Barbeque in a Biscuit

- 1 (10 ounce) package buttermilk biscuits
- 1 pound ground beef, lean
- 1 medium onion, finely chopped
- ½ cup ketchup
- 2 tablespoons light brown sugar
- 1 tablespoon cider vinegar
- ½ teaspoon chili powder
- 1 cup Cheddar cheese, grated

Separate dough into 10 biscuits and mold into 5-inch circles. Press each into the bottom and up the sides of a greased muffin tin; set aside. In a frying pan, brown ground beef and onion then drain if necessary. In a small bowl mix ketchup, brown sugar, vinegar and chili powder and stir until smooth. Add to beef mixture. Divide the beef mixture among biscuits in muffin cups, using about ¼ cup in each. Sprinkle with cheese. Bake at 375° for 15 to 20 minutes or until golden brown. Cool for about 5 minutes before removing from muffin tins.

# Beef Tenderloin and Blue Cheese Sauce

2-3 *pounds beef tenderloin*
½ *cup Worcestershire sauce*
*Fresh ground black pepper*

Bring tenderloin to room temperature, about ½ hour. Pour Worcestershire sauce over beef. Cover with fresh ground black pepper. Bake uncovered at 350° for about 30 to 40 minutes. After 30 minutes continue to check frequently so you do not overcook the meat. If you do not have a meat thermometer you can tell the tenderloin is done by sticking a metal skewer into the meat and then carefully putting it against your cheek. When the metal is warm, the meat is done. Remove the meat from the oven and let rest for 10 to 15 minutes before carving.

**Blue Cheese Sauce**

3 *tablespoons unsalted butter, softened*
4 *ounces blue cheese*
2 *cups beef broth*
1 *carrot, chopped*
1 *stalk celery, chopped*
3 *cloves garlic, crushed*
3 *tablespoons Madeira wine*
⅓ *cup of half & half*

Combine the butter and the Blue cheese. Form into 4 small balls and place into the refrigerator until firm. Combine the beef stock, carrot and celery. Bring to a boil. Take broth to a hard simmer and cook for 7 to 10 minutes or until broth is reduced to ½ cup. Strain broth to remove all carrot and celery. Set broth aside. In a medium saucepan sauté the garlic in the Madeira wine over medium heat, about 2 or 3 minutes. Add the beef broth. Cook 3 to 5 minutes until the liquid is reduced to ½ cup. Turn down the heat and slowly stir in the half & half. Simmer for about 5 minutes or until sauce is light brown in color. Stir in cheese balls one at a time until each has melted and sauce is free of lumps. Serve warm over the sliced tenderloin.

## Bouillabaisse

*1 cup finely chopped onion*
*½ cup margarine*
*2 (16 ounce) cans crushed tomatoes*
*1 (8 ounce) can tomato paste*
*2 cloves garlic, crushed*
*1 teaspoon salt*
*2 bay leaves*
*½ teaspoon black pepper*
*½ teaspoon crumbled basil*
*½ teaspoon hot pepper sauce*
*¼ teaspoon leaf thyme*
*1 (10 ounce) package frozen sliced okra*
*½ dozen clams in shell*
*1 dozen scallops*
*1 fillet of fish (mild and no bones)*
*1 pound fresh shelled shrimp*
*1 pint oysters (shucked)*
*Cooked rice (optional)*

Sauté onion in margarine for 3 to 4 minutes. Add next 9 ingredients. Bring to a boil and immediately turn to low heat. Add okra, cover and cook for approximately 10 minutes. Stir once or twice. Add clams, scallops and fish. Cover and cook over low heat until shells open. Add shrimp and oysters. Continue cooking for 5 to 8 minutes. Serve immediately. Serve in soup bowl with a spoonful of rice in middle or eat as is.

## Cheese-Olive Appetizers

*1 cup sharp cheese, grated*
*2 tablespoons margarine, melted*
*½ cup all-purpose flour*
*Salt and pepper to taste*
*½ teaspoon dry mustard*
*3 tablespoons water*
*Few drops Tabasco sauce*
*Few shakes paprika*
*1 (9 ounce) bottle olives, stuffed with pimento*

Drain olives. Mix all other ingredients until mixture can be handled. Mixture may need a little more flour or water - up to 1 cup flour may be used. Use about 1 teaspoon of mixture to wrap around each olive. Roll in palm of hand. These should be frozen on a cookie sheet, then stored in freezer containers until ready to use. Bake on cookie sheet at 450° for 20 minutes. Serve hot.

"Know the truth.
It will set you free."
(John 8:32)

## Chicken Enchiladas

- 1 *medium-sized onion, finely chopped*
- ¼ *pound sliced fresh mushrooms*
- 1 *tablespoon margarine*
- 3 *cups finely chopped cooked chicken breast*
- 1 *(10 ounce) can cream of mushroom soup, undiluted*
- 1 *(8 ounce) carton sour cream*
- 1 *(4 ounce) can chopped green chiles, drained*
- ½ *cup sliced almonds*
- ½ *teaspoon dried whole oregano*
- ¼ *teaspoon salt*
- ¼ *teaspoon pepper*
- 10 *(7 to 8 inch) flour tortillas*
- 1 *(10 ounce) can cream of chicken soup, undiluted*
- 1 *(12 ounce) jar medium picante salsa*
- 2 *cups (8 ounces) shredded sharp Cheddar cheese*

Sauté onions and mushrooms in margarine until tender. Combine chicken breasts, cream of mushroom soup, sour cream, chiles, almonds, oregano, salt and pepper; mix well. Spoon about ½ cup mixture in center of each tortilla; roll up and place seam side down in a lightly oiled 13x9x2-inch baking dish. Combine cream of chicken soup, picante salsa and grated cheese; spoon over tortillas. Bake uncovered at 350° for 30 to 35 minutes. Serve while hot.

# Chicken Lasagna Florentine

- 6-8 *lasagna noodles*
- 1 *(10 ounce) package frozen chopped spinach, thawed*
- 2 *cups chopped, cooked chicken*
- 1 *cup (8 ounces) shredded Cheddar cheese*
- ¼-½ *teaspoon ground nutmeg*
- ½ *teaspoon salt*
- ¼ *teaspoon pepper*
- 1 *tablespoon soy sauce*
- 1 *can cream of mushroom soup*
- 1 *(8 ounce) carton sour cream*
- 1 *(4.5 ounce) jar sliced mushrooms, drained*
- ⅓ *cup mayonnaise*
- ½ *cup Parmesan cheese*

Cook noodles; drain and set aside. Drain spinach well, pressing between layers of paper towels. Combine spinach, chicken and other ingredients in a large bowl; stir well. Arrange one layer of noodles in an 11x7-inch baking dish. Spread half of chicken mixture over noodles. Repeat procedure with remaining noodles and chicken. Sprinkle with Parmesan cheese and Butter-Pecan Topping. Bake, covered at 350° for 55 to 60 minutes. Let stand 10 to 15 minutes.

**Butter-Pecan Topping**

- 1 *cup pecans, chopped*
- 2 *tablespoons margarine*

Sauté 1 cup chopped pecans in 2 tablespoons margarine.

# Chicken Quiche

2 *tablespoons finely chopped onion*
2 *tablespoons sliced fresh mushrooms*
2 *tablespoons finely chopped bell pepper*
2 *tablespoons margarine*
1 *unbaked pie crust*
1 *cup cubed cooked chicken*
½ *cup (2 ounces) shredded Swiss cheese*
½ *cup (2 ounces) shredded sharp Cheddar cheese*
*Salt and pepper*
2 *eggs*
1 *teaspoon cornstarch*
¾ *cup half & half*
¾ *cup sour cream*

Sauté onion, mushrooms and bell pepper in margarine. Add to pie crust, then add chicken. Next, sprinkle on cheeses. Add salt and pepper if desired. Beat eggs; add cornstarch, half & half and sour cream. Mix well and pour over other ingredients. Bake at 400° for 10 minutes, reduce heat to 350° and bake for 30 to 35 minutes longer or until knife inserted in center comes out clean.

# Cider Punch

3 *cups apple juice*
2½ *cups unsweetened pineapple juice*
2 *cups cranberry juice*
¼ *cup brown sugar*
2 *cinnamon sticks*
2 *teaspoons whole cloves*
2 *teaspoons allspice*

Mix juice and sugar and pour into percolator coffeepot. In coffee basket, put spices. Perk and serve hot.

# Crab Bisque

- ½ cup butter
- ½ cup chopped onion
- 1 cup chopped green onion
- 4 cups chicken stock
- 4 carrots, minced
- 1 cup chopped parsley
- 2 cups chopped celery
- 3 teaspoons salt
- ½ teaspoon white pepper
- ½ teaspoon powdered mace
- ½ teaspoon thyme
- 3 bay leaves
- ¼ teaspoon hot pepper sauce
- 4 cups milk, divided
- ⅓ cup all-purpose flour
- 4 cups heavy cream
- 1 pound cleaned, cooked and chopped shrimp
- 1 pound lump crabmeat
- ½ teaspoon paprika

In large pot melt butter. Add onion and green onion and cook slowly until tender. Add chicken stock, carrots, parsley, celery, salt, pepper, mace, thyme, bay leaves and hot pepper sauce. Simmer for about 45 minutes, adding additional stock or water if necessary. Add 1 cup milk to flour, slowly mixing until smooth. Stir constantly and slowly add remaining milk and cream to the pot. Continue stirring over medium heat until smooth and thick. Reserve 3 tablespoons shrimp. Add remaining shrimp and crabmeat. Continue stirring and cook for 10 minutes more. Serve in large mugs or soup bowls. Garnish with chopped shrimp and paprika. Serves 12 to 14.

# Delicious Marinated Cheese

*1 (0.7 ounce) envelope Italian salad dressing mix*
*½ cup vegetable oil*
*¼ cup white vinegar*
*2 tablespoons water*
*2 tablespoons minced green onions*
*1½ teaspoons sugar*
*1 (8 ounce) package Monterey Jack cheese*
*1 (8 ounce) package sharp Cheddar cheese*
*1 (8 ounce) package cream cheese*
*1 (4 ounce) jar diced pimento, drained*
*Fresh parsley sprigs*

Combine first 6 ingredients in a small, tightly covered container. Shake vigorously to blend. Set aside. Cut Monterey Jack cheese crosswise into ¼-inch strips. Cut each strip in half to form 2 squares. Set aside. Cut Cheddar cheese and cream cheese using same directions. Arrange cheese slices like dominoes in several rows in a 2-quart dish, alternating Monterey Jack cheese, cream cheese and Cheddar cheese side by side. Pour marinade over cheeses. Cover and refrigerate for several hours or overnight. Drain and arrange cheese slices on a pretty serving dish. Top each row with diced pimento and garnish with fresh parsley sprigs. Serve with your best crackers. This is a wonderful appetizer.

## Deviled Pecan Ball

2 *(8 ounce) packages cream cheese, softened*
2 *cups (8 ounces) shredded sharp Cheddar cheese*
1 *(2¼ ounce) can deviled ham*
2 *tablespoons chopped pimento*
2 *teaspoons Worcestershire sauce*
2 *teaspoons grated onion*
1 *teaspoon dried parsley flakes*
1 *teaspoon lemon juice*
1 *teaspoon dry mustard*
¼ *teaspoon salt*
½ *teaspoon seasoned salt*
¾ *teaspoon paprika*
2-4 *drops hot pepper sauce*
2 *cups pecans, chopped*

Combine first 3 ingredients, blending well (I use mixer). Stir in remaining ingredients except pecans. Chill 2 hours. Divide cheese mixture in half and shape into 2 balls; roll in pecans. Serve with crackers.

## Easy Chicken Divan

- 2 *cups cooked chicken*
- 2 *cans cream of celery soup*
- 1 *small jar pimento*
- 1 *cup mayonnaise*
- ¾ *teaspoon curry powder*
- 1 *can mushrooms*
- *Juice of 1 lemon*
- 2 *(10 ounce) packages broccoli, cooked*
- *Italian breadcrumbs*

Cook and bone chicken. Combine chicken, soup, pimento, mayonnaise, curry powder, mushrooms and lemon juice. Pour over broccoli arranged in a 13x9x2-inch baking dish. Top with Italian breadcrumbs. Bake at 350° for about 30 minutes.

*I serve rice as a side dish with this.*

Never spend time or
effort trying to even the score.

## Fancy Chicken Log

- 2 (8 ounces) packages cream cheese, softened
- 1 tablespoon bottled steak sauce
- ½ teaspoon curry powder
- 1½ cups cooked chicken, minced
- ⅓ cup celery, minced
- ¼ cup parsley, chopped
- ¼ cup toasted almonds, chopped
- Round salted crackers

Beat together first 3 ingredients. Blend in next 2 ingredients and 2 tablespoons parsley. Mix well. Shape mixture into an 8 or 9-inch log. Wrap in aluminum foil and chill 4 to 6 hours, or overnight. Toss together remaining parsley and almonds and coat log in this mixture. Serve with round salted crackers. Makes about 3 cups spread.

"Make a joyful noise unto the Lord."
(Psalm 66:1-2)

# Hot Broccoli and Cheese Dip

- 1 *(10 ounce) package frozen chopped broccoli*
- 3 *ribs celery, chopped fine*
- ½ *large onion, chopped very fine*
- 1 *(4.5 ounce) jar of sliced mushrooms*
- 2 *tablespoons butter*
- 1 *($10\frac{3}{8}$ ounce) can cream of mushroom soup, undiluted*
- 1 *(6 ounce) roll soft garlic cheese*

Cook broccoli as directed and drain well. Sauté celery, onion and drained mushrooms in butter until tender. Add broccoli, soup and cheese. Combine well and heat through. Serve in chafing dish with large tortilla chips. Makes about 4 cups.

# Mango Chicken

- 8 *chicken breast halves*
- ¾-1 *cup sour cream*
- ¾-1 *cup mayonnaise*
- 1 *(9 ounce) jar Hot Mango Chutney*
- ½ *teaspoon cumin*
- ¾ *teaspoon curry*
- 1 *cup finely sliced celery*
- ½-1 *cup golden raisins (optional)*

Place chicken breasts in large pot and cover with water. Cook until chicken is very tender. Drain, then cut chicken into small (bite-size) pieces. Mix remaining ingredients and add to chicken. Stir until completely mixed. Place in covered refrigerator container and cool until about ½ hour before serving.

*The Hot Mango Chutney does not make this salad hot, just gives it a spicy taste. This is a great salad! Can be served on a lettuce leaf, in a scooped out tomato shell, or even on sandwich bread. Enjoy!*

## Marinated Mushrooms

*⅔ cup tarragon vinegar*
*½ cup salad oil*
*2 medium cloves garlic, halved*
*1 tablespoon sugar*
*1½ teaspoons salt*
*Fresh ground pepper*
*2 tablespoons water*
*Dash of Tabasco sauce*
*1 medium onion, thinly sliced in rings*
*2 quarts small fresh mushrooms*

Combine first 8 ingredients, putting garlic on toothpicks. Add onions and mushrooms. Cover and refrigerate for at least 8 hours, stirring several times. Remove toothpicks with garlic cloves and discard if you don't like garlic cloves in your food. This is great served over sliced tomatoes!

## Mexican Chicken

- 8 *chicken breast halves*
- 1 *package taco mix*
- 1 *can cream of chicken soup*
- 1 *cup grated Monterey Jack cheese (approximately 4 ounces)*
- 1 *cup sour cream*
- 1 *cup mild salsa*

Roll chicken breast halves in taco mix. Combine remaining ingredients except salsa. Place chicken breasts in a 9x13-inch baking pan and cover with soup mixture, then cover with salsa. Cover with aluminum foil or Saran Wrap and marinate in refrigerator for 2 hours. Remove cover and place in oven to bake at 350° until chicken is done, depending on the size of your chicken breast halves. Baking time should be about 30 to 45 minutes. Serve with a vegetable, salad and hot bread. Yum!

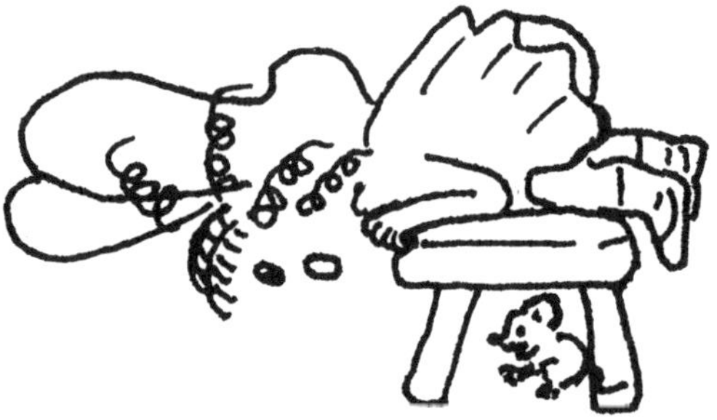

# Sauerkraut Balls

- ½ *pound of ground pork sausage*
- ¼ *cup chopped onion*
- 1 *(16 ounce) can of sauerkraut, chopped fine and drained*
- 2 *tablespoons unseasoned dry breadcrumbs*
- 1 *(3 ounce) package of cream cheese, softened*
- 1 *teaspoon prepared mustard*
- ¼ *teaspoon garlic salt*
- ¼ *teaspoon pepper*
- 2 *large eggs*
- ¼ *cup milk*
- ½ *cup flour*
- 1 *cup fine unseasoned breadcrumbs*

Crumble sausage into small pieces and sauté with chopped onion on medium heat until it just begins to lose the pink color. Remove from heat and drain well. Place drained sauerkraut between paper towels and press until it is very dry. Combine the sausage and sauerkraut mixtures. Stir in the 2 tablespoons of breadcrumbs. Beat the cream cheese until soft. Add the mustard, salt, garlic and pepper and mix until well blended. Add to your sausage-sauerkraut mixture and cover. Chill for at least 2 hours. Combine the milk and eggs in a bowl. Shape your sausage-sauerkraut mixture into 1-inch balls. Roll in the flour. Dip in the egg bath then roll in the dry breadcrumbs. Heat 2 inches of oil in a large skillet and fry. Continue to turn the balls until light golden brown, about 2 minutes. Drain on paper towels and serve warm with an assortment of mustards. The balls may be cooked and then frozen. To heat place the frozen balls on a cookie sheet and bake at 375° for about 10 minutes or until warm throughout.

## Southwest Chicken Casserole

- 1 (10 ounce) package yellow rice
- 1 cup chicken stock
- ⅓ stick margarine
- 1 medium onion, finely chopped
- 2 cups cooked chicken, finely chopped
- 1 tablespoon chili powder
- Salt and pepper to taste
- 1 (10 ounce) can cream of chicken soup
- 1 cup sour cream
- 1 (10 ounce) package Cheddar cheese, grated
- 1 (10 ounce) can tomatoes with green chiles (optional)

Cook rice in the chicken stock in a saucepan until tender. Sauté the onion in a skillet in small amount margarine until tender. Layer the rice, chicken and onion in a 9x13-inch baking dish. Add the chili powder, salt and pepper. Mix the soup and sour cream in a bowl. Spread over the casserole. Cover with the grated cheese. Top with the tomatoes. Bake at 350° for 30 minutes.

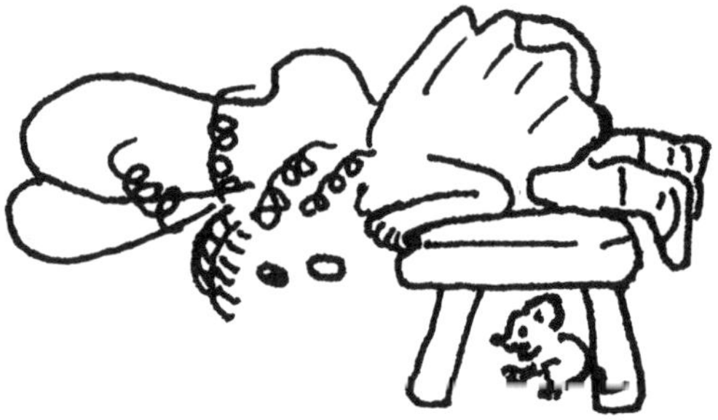

# Spinach-Ricotta Pie

- 1 *teaspoon butter or margarine*
- 1 *cup minced onion*
- 1 *cup sliced fresh mushrooms*
- 1 *pound spinach, stemmed and chopped*
- ½ *teaspoon salt*
- *Pepper, freshly ground and to taste*
- 1 *teaspoon basil*
- 1 *pound ricotta cheese*
- 3 *eggs, beaten*
- 3 *tablespoons all-purpose flour*
- ¾ *cup grated cheese of your choice*
- *Nutmeg (dash)*
- *Paprika (dash)*
- *Unbaked pie shell (crust)*
- 1 *cup sour cream*

Preheat oven to 375°. Melt butter or margarine in skillet. Add onion and mushrooms. Sauté for 5 minutes over medium heat. Add spinach, salt, pepper and basil. Cook, stirring, over medium heat until spinach is wilted. Remove from heat. Drain any remaining liquid. Combine remaining filling ingredients, except sour cream, in a large bowl and mix well. Add spinach to filling ingredients and spread into unbaked pie shell. Top with sour cream, spread to the edges of the crust. Dust with paprika. Bake for 40 to 45 minutes or until firm when you insert knife into center and it comes out clean.

## Taco Cheesecake

- 4 *cups crushed tortilla chips*
- 3 *tablespoons butter or margarine, melted*
- 1 *pound ground lean beef*
- 1 *(1.25 ounce) envelope taco seasoning mix, divided*
- 2 *tablespoons water*
- 2 *(8 ounce) packages cream cheese, softened*
- 2 *large eggs*
- 2 *cups (8 ounces) sharp Cheddar cheese, shredded*
- 1 *(8 ounce) container sour cream*
- 2 *tablespoons all-purpose flour*
- 3 *toppings: shredded lettuce, chopped tomato, chopped green bell pepper*

Stir together crushed tortilla chips and butter; press into bottom of a 9-inch springform pan. Bake at 325° for 10 minutes. Cool on wire rack. Cook beef in a large skillet over medium heat, stirring until it crumbles and is no longer pink; drain and pat dry with paper towels. Return beef to skillet. Reserve 1 teaspoon taco seasoning mix. Stir remaining taco mix and 2 tablespoons water into beef. Cook over medium heat, stirring occasionally for about 4 to 5 minutes. Beat cream cheese at a medium speed with an electric mixer until fluffy; add eggs and reserved 1 teaspoon taco seasoning mix, beating until blended. Add Cheddar cheese; beat until well mixed. Spread cream cheese mixture evenly over crust and 1-inch up sides of pan. Spoon in beef mixture. Spread cream cheese mixture from around sides of pan over beef mixture forming a 1-inch border. Combine sour cream and flour; spread over cheesecake. Bake at 325° for 25 minutes. Cool in pan on a wire rack for 10 minutes. Run a knife around the edge to release sides from pan. Serve warm with toppings. Store unused cheesecake in refrigerator.

# Tides Road Dip

8 *ounces cream cheese, room temperature*
4 *ounces crumbled blue cheese*
½ *teaspoon Tabasco sauce*
½ *teaspoon Worcestershire sauce*
½ *teaspoon granulated garlic*

Combine all ingredients and refrigerate at least one day for best flavor. Serve on crackers.

## Vidalia Onion Dip

*1 cup mayonnaise*
*1 cup finely chopped Vidalia onions*
*1 cup grated Parmesan cheese*

Combine all ingredients and put into a greased shallow baking dish. Bake at 325° for 30 to 35 minutes until bubbly. Serve with crackers and chips.

"Whosoever" in God's Word
means me! Take it personally.
(John 3:16)

## Christmas Made Special

Try to find a place where your family can go together to cut down your own Christmas tree. If this is not possible take the whole family along to a tree lot to help choose your special tree.

When we were kids we always went out to our ranch with our grandfather during the summer and chose "our" tree for Christmas time. It always had to be the most beautiful tree we could find.

Several days before Christmas, Papa (our wonderful grandfather) loaded us up in the back of his truck and off we went to cut down our special tree. Usually it was there waiting for us, but on more than one occasion someone had sneaked out on the ranch and stolen our tree. We were heartbroken at first, but somehow, Papa always managed to lead us to another almost perfect tree. He cut the tree down and we helped him load it on his truck. We laughed and sang at the top of our voices all the way home where our mother and grandmother waited for the special tree (A wonderful, happy memory.)

On Christmas Day we always had a huge, wonderfully baked fresh turkey, hot and mild corn bread dressing, delicious gravy, conch peas with hot pepper sauce, fresh fruit salad, roasted pecans, cranberry sauce, celery stuffed with cream cheese and pecan slivers, slavery bread, fresh coconut cake, plain pound cake (for Papa), pecan and pumpkin pies and ambrosia.

Everyone always waddled away from the table in absolute misery from eating too much. Everyone except Papa. He was always the one with the self-control. He was able to leave one bite of food on his plate if he was full, or happily refuse dessert. Not the rest of us. We stuffed ourselves and were miserable. I always admired my grandfather's self-control, but never could understand how he could turn down a yummy dessert.

Gather close my precious grandchildren,
Gather close around my knee.
Let me tell you about our Saviour,
And the joy He has brought to me

# Christmas

"'Twas the night before Jesus came and all through the house
Not a creature was praying, not one in the house.
Their Bibles were lain on the shelf without care
In hopes that Jesus would not come there.
The children were dressing to crawl into bed
Not once ever kneeling or bowing a head.
And Mom in her rocker with baby on her lap
Was watching the Late Show while I took a nap.
When out of the East there arose such a clatter,
I sprang to my feet to see what was the matter.
Away to the window I flew like a flash
Tore open the shutters and threw up the sash!
When what to my wondering eyes should appear
But angels proclaiming that Jesus was here.
With a light like the sun sending forth a bright ray
I knew in a moment this must be The Day!
The light of His face made me cover my head
It was Jesus! Returning just like He had said.
And though I possessed worldly wisdom and wealth
I cried when I saw Him in spite of myself.
In the Book of Life which He held in His hand
Was written the name of every saved man.
He spoke not a word as He searched for my name;
When He said, "It's not here", my head hung in shame.
The people whose names had been written with love
He gathered to take to His Father above.
With those who were ready He rose without a sound
While all the rest were left standing around.
I fell to my knees, but it was too late;
I had waited too long and this sealed my fate.
I stood and I cried as they rose out of sight;
Oh, if only I had been ready tonight.
In the words of this poem the meaning is clear;
The coming of Jesus is drawing near.
There's only one life and when comes the last call
We'll find that the Bible was true after all!

Author Unknown

# Christmas Morning

Christmas Morning is a happy and exciting time as you have a special breakfast together, then begin opening gifts. Most of these recipes are perfect for Christmas Morning. We usually have Breakfast Lasagna and Baked Sausage Grits.

## Applesauce Muffins

2 *sticks margarine*
2 *cups sugar*
2 *eggs, well beaten*
1 *teaspoon vanilla*
4 *cups all-purpose flour*
1 *tablespoon baking soda*
1 *teaspoon cloves*
1 *teaspoon allspice*
1 *teaspoon cinnamon*
1 *cup white raisins*
1 *cup chopped pecans*
3 *cups applesauce*

Mix together margarine and sugar in large mixing bowl until smooth. Add eggs and vanilla. Sift flour, soda and spices; then add to margarine mixture. Add raisins, pecans and applesauce and mix until all ingredients are smooth. Bake in greased muffin tins at 400° for about 15 minutes or until brown.

*This makes a large number of muffins and will keep in refrigerator up to 2 weeks. Good warmed over, sliced and topped with butter or cream cheese. Baking times depend on size of your muffin cups. Do not overbake.*

## Baked Cheese Grits

*1 cup grits, coarse if possible*
*4 cups water*
*1 teaspoon salt*
*1 stick margarine*
*2 eggs, beaten*
*1¼ cups (5 ounces) grated Cheddar cheese, divided*

Combine grits, water and salt. Cook over low heat for about 20 minutes, stirring often. Keep pot covered or the grits will pop out on you. Remove from heat, add margarine and stir until completely melted. Add eggs and 1 cup cheese. Pour into casserole dish and top with ¼ cup cheese. Bake at 350° for 20 to 30 minutes. Serves 6 to 8.

What You do is what You believe.
All the rest is JUST TALK!

## Breakfast Lasagna

*16 slices white bread*
*1½ pounds ham, sliced*
*16 ounces (4 cups) 4 cheese Mexican blend*
*8 eggs*
*2 cups milk*
*¾ teaspoon dry mustard*
*½ teaspoon onion salt*
*1½ sticks butter*
*3 cups corn flakes, crushed*

Remove crust from bread. Layer in a 13x9x2-inch baking dish: bread, ham, 2 cups grated cheese. Repeat. In a blender, add eggs, milk, mustard and onion salt; blend. Pour egg mixture over ham and cheese layers and refrigerate overnight. This is a must! About ½ hour before baking, remove from refrigerator. Heat oven to 350°. Melt butter and mix with enough corn flakes to cover top cheese layer. Bake for about 30 minutes. Serves 12.

*A delicious Christmas breakfast!*

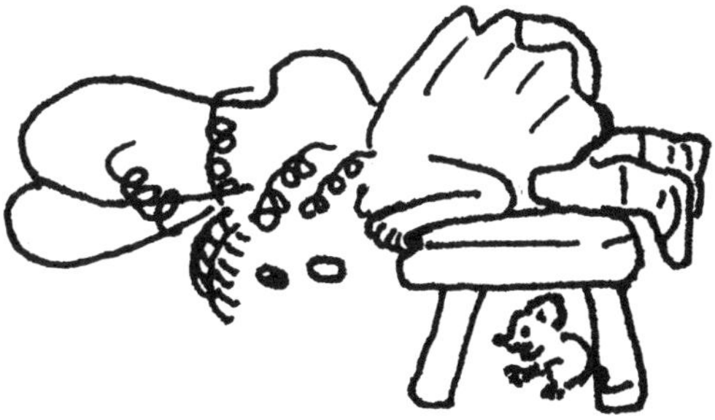

# French Toast Casserole

| | | | |
|---|---|---|---|
| *1½* | *sticks butter* | *6* | *eggs* |
| *1½* | *cups brown sugar* | *3* | *cups milk* |
| *1* | *tablespoon cinnamon* | *⅓* | *cup white sugar* |
| *18* | *slices of bread (thickly sliced)* | | *Powdered sugar* |

Melt butter and add brown sugar and cinnamon. Spread a layer of the mixture on the bottom of a 9x13-inch pan. Then layer bread and the rest of the sugar mixture. Mix the eggs, milk, and white sugar and pour over bread. Refrigerate overnight. Bake at 350° for 30 minutes and sprinkle with powdered sugar.

Call a family member or a friend today and let them know that you miss them, and especially that you love them!

# Fresh Blueberry Coffee Cake

*1¼ cups fresh blueberries*
*⅓ cup sugar*
*2 tablespoons cornstarch*
*¼ cup butter or margarine, softened*
*1 cup sugar*
*2 eggs*
*2 cups all-purpose flour*
*1 teaspoon baking powder*
*1 teaspoon baking soda*
*½ teaspoon salt*
*1 (8 ounce) carton sour cream*
*1 teaspoon almond extract*
*½ cup finely chopped pecans*

Combine blueberries, ⅓ cup sugar and cornstarch in small saucepan. Cook over low heat 2 to 3 minutes or until sauce is thickened, stirring constantly. Set sauce aside. Cream butter; gradually add 1 cup sugar, beating until well blended. Add eggs, 1 at a time, beating well after each. Combine flour, baking powder, baking soda and salt; add to creamed mixture alternately with sour cream, beginning and ending with flour mixture. Stir in almond extract. Spoon half of batter into a greased 8-inch fluted tube pan; spoon on half the blueberry sauce, swirling partially through batter with a knife. Repeat with the remaining batter and blueberry sauce. Sprinkle with pecans. Bake at 350° for 50 minutes or until done. Let stand 5 minutes before removing from pan. Place coffee cake on serving plate. Makes 1 (8-inch) coffee cake.

# Gingerbread Muffins

*1 cup margarine*
*1½ cups sugar*
*4 eggs*
*1 cup molasses*
*1 (8 ounce) carton sour cream*
*4 cups all-purpose flour*
*2 teaspoons baking soda*
*1 teaspoon baking powder*
*3 teaspoons ground ginger*
*¼ teaspoon allspice*
*¼ teaspoon cinnamon*
*1 cup dark raisins*
*1 cup pecans, chopped*

Cream margarine; gradually add the sugar, beating until light and fluffy. Add eggs, 1 at a time, beating well after each. Add molasses and mix well. Add sour cream and mix well. Combine remaining ingredients and mix together well. Add gradually to batter, stirring with a large spoon. Stir until all ingredients are moistened. Fill greased (prepared with nonstick vegetable spray) muffin tins about ½ full. Bake in 400° oven for approximately 10 minutes or until lightly browned. Do not overbake.

*These are also great baked in miniature muffin tins but do not overbake.*

## Grits-Sausage Bake

- 1 *pound hot sausage*
- 1 *small onion, finely chopped*
- 1 *cup yellow grits*
- 4 *cups water*
- ½ *stick margarine*
- 4 *large eggs, beaten*
- ½ *cup (2 ounces) grated hot pepper cheese*
- 1 *cup (4 ounces) grated sharp Cheddar cheese, divided*

Crumble sausage, brown with onion and drain completely. Cook grits in water for 15 to 20 minutes, stirring frequently. Add margarine, eggs (or egg substitute), pepper cheese and ½ cup Cheddar cheese. Add well-drained sausage and onion. Pour into baking dish and top with remaining Cheddar cheese. Bake in microwave on medium heat for 3 to 5 minutes or until bubbly. Or bake in conventional oven at 300° for 20 minutes. Can be made day ahead, stored in refrigerator and baked just before serving. Serves 6.

## Monkey Bread

- ½ cup pecans, chopped
- ½ cup sugar
- 1 teaspoon ground cinnamon
- 3 (10 ounce) cans refrigerated buttermilk biscuits
- 1 cup firmly packed brown sugar
- ½ cup butter or margarine, melted

Sprinkle pecans in the bottom of a well-greased 10-inch Bundt pan. Combine sugar and cinnamon. Cut biscuits into quarters and roll each piece in sugar mixture. Layer in pan. Combine brown sugar and butter, pour over dough. Bake at 350° for 30 to 40 minutes. Cool bread for 10 minutes in pan, then invert on a pretty plate. Just pull off a section, and enjoy.

*This is a must at our house on Thanksgiving, Christmas and Easter.*

"Do not neglect to show hospitality."
(Hebrews 13:2)

## Morning Glory Muffins

- 2 *cups all-purpose flour*
- ½ *cup whole wheat flour*
- 1 *cup packed brown sugar*
- 2 *teaspoons baking soda*
- 2 *teaspoons cinnamon*
- ½ *teaspoon salt*
- 2 *cups shredded carrots*
- 1 *cup shredded apple (like Granny Smith)*
- 1 *cup raisins*
- 1 *(8 ounce) can crushed pineapple, drained*
- *Nuts, such as pecans (optional)*
- ⅓ *cup vegetable oil*
- ⅓ *cup apple butter*
- 2 *teaspoons vanilla extract*
- 3 *eggs*

Preheat oven to 350°. Spoon flours into measuring cups and level with a knife. Combine brown sugar, baking soda, cinnamon, and salt into the flour. Stir in carrot, apple, raisins, and pineapple (and nuts, if used). Mix thoroughly; batter will be thin. In another bowl, combine oil, apple butter, vanilla, and eggs with a whisk. Add this into the center of the flour mixture and mix until moist. Grease 2 dozen muffin cups and spoon in batter. Bake for 20 to 25 minutes. Remove muffins from pans and cool on wire rack. Makes 2 dozen.

## Peanut Butter Coffee Cake

- *1½ cups firmly-packed brown sugar, divided*
- *2½ cups all-purpose flour, divided*
- *¾ cup peanut butter, divided*
- *4 tablespoons margarine, melted*
- *¼ cup shortening*
- *2 eggs*
- *2 teaspoons baking powder*
- *½ teaspoon baking soda*
- *½ teaspoon salt*
- *1 cup milk*

In mixing bowl, stir together ½ cup brown sugar, ½ cup flour, ¼ cup peanut butter and melted margarine until crumbly; set aside. Cream ½ cup peanut butter and shortening. Gradually beat in 1 cup brown sugar until light and fluffy. Add eggs, 1 at a time, stirring well after each. Stir together 2 cups flour, baking powder, baking soda and salt. Add flour mixture and milk alternately to creamed mixture, mixing well after each addition. Turn mixture into greased 13x9x2-inch baking pan. Sprinkle with crumbly topping. Bake in 375° oven for 30 to 35 minutes or until done. Makes 1 coffee cake.

## Sausage and Egg Bake

*1 pound sausage*
*4 slices bread, cubed*
*1¼ cups (5 ounces) grated sharp Cheddar cheese, divided*
*8 large eggs*
*1 cup milk*
*Salt and pepper*
*1 small can sliced mushrooms, drained*

Cook sausage thoroughly and drain, leaving chunky. Place bread cubes on bottom of 12x9x2-inch dish. Add sausage and ½ of cheese. Beat eggs, milk, salt and pepper together and pour over sausage. Top with rest of cheese and mushrooms. Bake at 325° for 40 to 45 minutes.

*May be made ahead and stored in refrigerator until ready to bake next morning. I use hot sausage but mild or sage sausage is good too.*

"Give thanks to Him and praise His name."
(Psalms 100:4)

## Strawberry-Cream Cheese Coffee Cake

*1 (3 ounce) package cream cheese*
*4 tablespoons butter or margarine*
*2 cups packaged biscuit mix*
*⅓ cup whole milk, room temperature*
*½ cup strawberry jam or preserves*
*1 cup sifted confectioners' sugar*
*1-2 tablespoons milk*
*½ teaspoon vanilla*

Cut cream cheese and butter or margarine into biscuit mix until crumbly. Blend in the ⅓ cup milk. Turn onto floured surface; knead 10 to 12 times. On waxed paper roll dough to 12x8-inch rectangle. Turn onto greased baking sheet; remove paper. Spread jam or preserves down center of dough. Make 2½-inch cuts at 1-inch intervals on long sides. Fold strips over filling. Bake in 425° oven for 12 to 15 minutes. Combine sugar, remaining milk and vanilla. Drizzle on top. Serve warm.

"Pray without ceasing."
(I Thessalonians 5:17)

# Strawberry Cream Cheese Coffeecake

*2½ cups all-purpose flour*
*¾ cup sugar*
*¾ cup margarine*
*½ teaspoon baking powder*
*½ teaspoon baking soda*
*¼ teaspoon salt*
*¾ cup sour cream*
*1 egg*
*1 teaspoon almond extract*
*1 (8 ounce) package cream cheese, room temperature*
*¼ cup sugar*
*1 egg*
*½ cup strawberry preserves*
*½ cup sliced almonds, pecans or walnuts*

Grease and flour bottom and sides of a 9 to 10-inch springform pan. In large bowl, combine flour and ¾ cup sugar. Using pastry blender cut in margarine until it resembles coarse crumbs. Reserve 1 cup. To remaining crumb mixture, add baking powder, baking soda, salt, sour cream, 1 egg and almond extract; blend well. Spread batter on bottom and 2-inches up sides of pan. In a small bowl, combine cream cheese, ¼ cup sugar and 1 egg; blend well. Pour over batter in pan. Carefully spoon preserves evenly over cheese filling. In another small bowl, combine 1 cup reserved crumb mixture and nuts. Sprinkle over top. Bake until cream cheese filling is set and crust is deep golden brown. (You can use a 9x13-inch baking pan if you don't have a springform pan.) Cool 15 to 30 minutes, then refrigerate.

## Swedish Pancakes

- ½ *cup all-purpose flour*
- ½ *teaspoon salt*
- 3 *tablespoons sugar*
- ½ *cup milk*
- 1 *egg*

Mix dry ingredients, add milk slowly, stir until smooth. Add egg and beat thoroughly. Cook on hot griddle or frying pan. Make thin pancakes that can be rolled and filled with jelly or jam, or topped with butter and syrup.

Keep in close touch with your children and grandchildren. We may not always like the way they live or what they do, but we do always love them. Letting them know that we love them, no matter what, is probably one of the most important things that we can do for them, and for your relationship with them.

## Gravy for Turkey and Dressing

*1 quart turkey or chicken broth*
*3 tablespoons cornstarch*
*Chicken giblets from boiled wings, necks, etc.*

Heat but do not boil chicken broth. In a small bowl with 3 tablespoons cornstarch, add a few sprinkles of salt and ½ cup chicken or turkey broth. Stir until smooth then slowly add to pot of chicken broth. Stir often until thickened. If this is not thick enough add 1 tablespoon cornstarch with few sprinkles of salt and ¼ cup broth. When completely combined slowly add to broth and stir. Stir often to thicken, but DO NOT BOIL. Serve with turkey and dressing. (I'm hungry just thinking about it!)

*I always have to stew 3 to 4 chickens before Christmas to have enough broth for gravy and the dressing. I use the chicken for chicken and rice casseroles or chicken enchiladas, etc. to have in the freezer for company.*

## Ambrosia

*1 dozen large navel oranges*
*3 large bananas*
*1 cup grated coconut*

Peel oranges and section. Peel bananas, chop and immediately add to oranges, stirring lightly to keep bananas from turning brown. Add coconut, stir and refrigerate in covered container until ready to serve.

*Other fruit can be added, if desired.*

# Apple-Walnut Cake

*1 can apple pie filling*
*2 cups all-purpose flour*
*1 cup sugar*
*1½ teaspoons baking soda*
*1 teaspoon salt*
*2 eggs, beaten*
*1 teaspoon vanilla*
*⅔ cup vegetable oil*
*1 cup walnuts, chopped, divided*
*Sour Cream Topping*

Spread pie filling in bottom of a 13x9-inch pan. Combine flour, sugar, baking soda and salt; sprinkle over pie filling. In mixing bowl combine eggs, vanilla, oil and ¾ cup walnuts; mix well. Pour over ingredients in baking pan. Stir only until blended well. Smooth batter evenly in pan. Bake at 350° for 45 minutes. Remove from oven. Stick small holes in cake with a fork. Pour hot Sour Cream Topping over warm cake and sprinkle with ¼ cup walnuts. Serve warm or cold, cut into squares.

**Sour Cream Topping**

*1 cup sugar*
*½ cup sour cream*
*½ teaspoon baking soda*

Combine ingredients in saucepan. Cook over low heat, stirring constantly, until mixture comes to a boil. Immediately remove from heat and pour over warm cake.

*Watch carefully or topping will burn.*

## Baked Rice

- 1 *stick margarine*
- 1 *cup uncooked long grain rice*
- 1 *large onion, very finely minced*
- 1 *small can mushrooms, drained*
- 1 *can water chestnuts, drained and sliced*
- 2 *cans beef consommé*

Melt margarine in 8x8-inch casserole dish. Put rice over melted margarine. Sprinkle onions over rice, then mushrooms and water chestnuts. Pour consommé over top. Bake uncovered at 350° for 1 hour. DO NOT STIR.

*I use fresh mushrooms. Slice and sauté in pan prepared with nonstick vegetable spray for about 5 to 10 minutes, then add to recipe.*

"Whatsoever you do, do it heartily."
(Colossians 3:23)

## Blueberry Salad

- 2 *(3 ounce) packages blackberry gelatin*
- 2 *cups boiling water*
- 1 *(20 ounce) can crushed pineapple*
- 1 *can blueberry pie filling*
- 2 *cups sour cream*
- 1 *(8 ounce) package cream cheese*
- ¼ *cup sugar*
- ½ *teaspoon vanilla*
- ¼ *cup chopped pecans*

Mix gelatin with boiling water, then add crushed pineapple with juice and pie filling. Mix all together. Refrigerate in oblong 13x9x2-inch baking dish. Mix sour cream, cream cheese, sugar and vanilla, then spread on top of hardened gelatin. Sprinkle with chopped pecans.

Pray for someone who is not on your "good" list…doesn't matter why. Keep praying daily for this person or persons and you will soon see major changes…either in you or the other person. God does answer prayer!

## Brazil Nut Sticks

*1 pound Brazil nuts in shells or ½ pound shelled*
*1¾ cups all-purpose flour*
*1 teaspoon baking powder*
*2 eggs*
*2 cups light brown sugar*

Grind nuts; add to flour sifted with baking powder. Beat sugar into well-beaten eggs. Fold flour and nuts into egg mixture. Chill dough. Shape dough into finger-sized sticks. Bake at 350° for 10 minutes. Let ripen in tightly closed container for 2 to 3 weeks before eating.

*There was just no way we could have Thanksgiving and Christmas without these. Mother never let us even touch them before they had ripened for at least 2 weeks.*

# Broccoli and Cheese Salad

**Dressing**

½ *cup mayonnaise*

1 *tablespoon sugar*

3 *tablespoons red wine vinegar*

*Dash of salt*

**Salad**

2 *bunches of chopped broccoli*

½ *pound of cooked bacon, crumbled*

½ *cup finely chopped yellow onion*

8 *ounces cubed Cheddar cheese*

Combine all the ingredients of your dressing, stirring well. Add all remaining ingredients and chill for at least 2 hours before serving.

## Broccoli Casserole

2 *packages broccoli, chopped, cooked and drained*
2 *cans chicken-mushroom soup*
⅔ *cup milk*
2 *cans onion rings*
2 *cups sharp Cheddar cheese, grated*
*Cooking spray*

Cook broccoli. While it is cooking, spray Pyrex rectangular dish. Mix soup and milk. Add broccoli, 1 can onion rings and 2 cups grated cheese. Pour into dish. Top with remaining can of onion rings. Bake at 350° for 30 minutes.

*Recipe is easily divided.*

"Do not be frightened or dismayed, for the Lord your God is with you wherever you go."
(Joshua 1:9)

# Chicken Casserole

- 1 (16 ounce) package Pepperidge Farms stuffing mix
- 1 stick margarine or butter, melted
- 1 cup water
- 2½ cups cooked chicken breast, cut into pieces
- ½ cup celery, finely chopped
- ¼ cup green onions, finely chopped
- 4 ounces sliced mushrooms, drained
- ½ cup sliced almonds
- ½ cup mayonnaise (real, not lite or fat-free)
- 2 eggs, slightly beaten
- 1½ cups milk
- 1 can cream of mushroom soup
- ½-1 cup sharp cheese, grated

Combine stuffing mix, margarine and water. Spread ½ in a buttered 9x12-inch baking dish. Combine chicken breasts, celery, green onions, mushrooms, almonds and mayonnaise. Spread over dressing mix in baking dish. Cover with remaining stuffing mix. Mix eggs and milk. Pour evenly over chicken mixture. Cover and refrigerate overnight. Remove from refrigerator 1 hour before baking and spread mushroom soup over top. Bake uncovered at 325° for 40 minutes. Sprinkle with cheese and bake an additional 10 minutes. Serve warm.

# Chocolate Fondue

- *1 cup semi-sweet chocolate chips*
- *½ cup evaporated milk*
- *¼ cup marshmallow cream*

Put all in the fondue pot at 200° and stir occasionally until color is dark.

*Great for dip - use strawberries, pound cake cubes, banana slices, pineapple chunks, pecan halves, etc.*

We are responsible for what we do, no matter how we feel.

# Thank You Father

If ever a person was blessed,

It surely has to be me.

A father who adored me,

A mother who thinks I am wonderful,

A husband who loves and cares for me,

Three daughters who think I am great,

A son who loves me,

Two wonderful sons in law,

Eight grandchildren who think I am special,

A sister who loves me and thinks I am better than I am,

Many wonderful friends who really care about me,

And most of all a Heavenly Father
who loves and watches over me every day,

And helps my family to see me through His forgiving eyes.

Thank you, Father. I adore you!

*Jeannine B. Browning*

# Christmas Punch

**Ice Ring**

*Water to fill mold*
*Cherries*
*Mint leaves*

Several days before Christmas add above ingredients to round mold and freeze. Water can be colored with food coloring, if you want a red or green mold.

*To be taken out of freezer and placed in punch bowl with punch.*

**Punch**

1 *large package frozen, sliced strawberries*
1 *large container frozen berry juice concentrate*
2 *(2 liter) bottles of ginger ale or lemon-lime soda*

Combine all and place in punch bowl. Add ice ring and serve.

*Other juices can be used according to your preference.*

# Cranberry Salad

- *1 package fresh cranberries*
- *1 whole seedless orange, chopped*
- *1 cup hot water*
- *1 envelope clear gelatin*
- *1 package lemon Jell-O*
- *½-¾ cup sugar (to taste)*
- *1 cup pecans, chopped*
- *1 cup crushed pineapple, drained*

Grind cranberries and add to chopped orange. Boil water and dissolve gelatin and lemon Jell-O. Add all other ingredients and mix well. Place in serving dish and refrigerate overnight. Cut into serving pieces and serve on fancy lettuce leaves.

"I can do all things through Christ who strengthens me."
(Philippians 4:13)

# Cream Cheese Frosted Melon

- *1 package lime (or other flavor) gelatin*
- *¾ cup boiling water*
- *¾ cup cold water*
- *1 medium cantaloupe*
- *2 dozen or so green grapes (or fresh berries)*
- *2-3 (3 ounce) packages cream cheese*
- *2 tablespoons (about) milk*
- *1 tablespoon powdered sugar*

Dissolve gelatin in boiling water. Add cold water. Peel melon, leaving it whole. Cut and save a slice from one end, scoop out seeds and drain well. Fill melon with water, then pour water in cup to measure capacity (discard water). Measure an equal amount of gelatin with fruit into melon (save and chill remaining gelatin for another meal). Keeping melon upright in bowl, chill in refrigerator until gelatin is set. Also chill and save end slice of melon. Once the gelatin is set replace cut slice by fastening with toothpicks. Blend cream cheese, powdered sugar and milk until smooth and fluffy. Turn melon on its side and cut a thin slice from one side for a firm base and place on a platter. If melon is very moist, pat dry top and sides with paper towel. Spread cream cheese over melon. Add grape halves as decoration. Place back in refrigerator just until time to slice and serve (remember to remove toothpicks). Makes about 6 servings.

*Can also use honeydew melon with strawberry gelatin and strawberries (fruit).*

# Deviled Eggs Supreme

- 6 *hard-boiled eggs*
- ¾ *cup mayonnaise*
- ½-¾ *teaspoon Creole seasoning (or to taste)*
- ¼ *teaspoon garlic powder*
- ½ *teaspoon yellow mustard*
- 6 *large green olives*

Boil eggs, cool, peel and cut in half lengthwise. Remove yellow centers and place in small bowl. Mash until all lumps are gone, then add remaining ingredients and mix well. Spoon yellow egg mixture into the white halves of the eggs. Top with a thick slice of green olive. These are great as an appetizer or with meals.

# Fresh Fruit Salad

3 *firm, yellow bananas, sliced*
1 *can pineapple chunks, juice saved*
1 *red apple, diced*
1 *yellow apple, diced*
1 *bottle cherries, drained*
1 *can Mandarin oranges, sliced, drained*
2 *cups seedless grapes*

Peel and slice bananas and immediately pour pineapple chunks and juice over them. This will keep the bananas from turning brown. Add remaining ingredients, store in refrigerator in covered container. When ready to use, drain juice. Needs no dressing.

*Watermelon, cantaloupe, blueberries, etc. can be added when available.*

Either you control your attitude, or it controls you! Keep a smile on your face!

# Squash Casserole

*6-7 yellow squash, washed and sliced*
*1 large onion, minced*
*Salt and pepper to taste*
*1 egg*
*1 stick margarine, melted*
*1 (8 ounce) package sharp Cheddar cheese, grated*
*½-1 cup garlic croutons*

Cook squash and onion in water to cover with salt and pepper. Cook until just tender. Drain well. Combine egg and margarine, add to squash. Combine cheese and garlic croutons, stir into squash and pour into casserole dish. Bake at 350° for 25 to 30 minutes.

"Perfect love casts out all fear."
(I John 4:18)

## Marinated Mushrooms and Olives

- *½ cup tarragon vinegar*
- *1 (9 ounce) jar green pimento stuffed whole olives, drained and liquid reserved*
- *¼ cup oil*
- *1 clove garlic, minced*
- *1 teaspoon oregano*
- *3 (6 ounce) jars whole mushrooms, drained*

Mix vinegar, olive liquid, oil, garlic and oregano; add mushrooms and olives. Marinate at least overnight. Drain and serve. A delicious appetizer.

# Holiday Pasta Salad

- 2 *cups Newman's Own Oil and Vinegar salad dressing*
- 2 *cups ranch dressing (regular, not light)*

Mix well and reserve for salad. If you should have any left over, the combination of these two dressings makes a great salad dressing.

- 3 *(6 ounce) jars sliced mushrooms*
- 1 *(9 ounce) jar green olives, whole, drained and liquid reserved*
- ½ *cup tarragon vinegar*
- ¼ *cup oil*
- 1 *clove garlic, minced*
- 1 *teaspoon oregano*

Mix vinegar, olive liquid, oil, garlic and oregano; add mushrooms and olives. Marinate at least overnight.

*This is also a wonderful appetizer. Use whole mushrooms instead of sliced ones. Everyone loves them.*

- 1 *(8 ounce) package pasta (your choice, but colored if possible)*
- 1 *medium red bell pepper, diced*
- 1 *medium green bell pepper, diced*
- 1 *medium sweet onion, thinly sliced (optional)*
- 1 *cup frozen small English peas, uncooked*
- 1 *(2 ounce) jar chopped pimento, drained*
- ½ *(12 ounce) jar mild banana pepper rings*

Cook pasta according to directions on package, but do not overcook. Drain and rinse. Add all remaining ingredients. Stir until completely mixed. Enjoy! This will keep in refrigerator for about 2 weeks, but it won't last that long if you have many pasta lovers.

*Grilled chicken or baked ham can be added to your pasta salad to make it a meal.*

*This looks like a lot of ingredients and a lot of trouble, but you can have the salad made in approximately 30 minutes. And besides, it is worth all the time and effort you put into it. Everyone loves this salad!*

## Karl's Potato Casserole

- 8 *large baking potatoes*
- 1 *pound sliced American cheese, cut into strips*
- 1 *cup mayonnaise*
- ½ *cup finely chopped onions*
- *Salt and pepper*
- ½ *pound par-cooked bacon, chopped*
- ¼ *cup stuffed green olives, chopped*

Wash and quarter the potatoes. Par boil for about 10 to 15 minutes. The potatoes should be barely fork tender and firm. Rinse under cold water to stop the cooking process. Allow to cool. Peel and cut into large bite-size pieces. Place potatoes into a large greased casserole dish. Combine the mayonnaise, ½ the cheese, onion, salt and pepper. Mix with the potatoes. Top with remaining cheese, bacon and olives. Bake at 325° for 1 hour.

# Layered Corn Bread

- *1 cup yellow cream corn meal*
- *1 cup Parmesan cheese (fat free)*
- *1 teaspoon baking powder*
- *1 teaspoon salt*
- *2 eggs*
- *1 cup sour cream (fat free)*
- *½ cup vegetable oil*
- *1 cup bacon bits (or real bacon, fried, blotted and chopped)*
- *1 can cream style corn*
- *1 cup sharp Cheddar cheese, grated*

Combine corn meal, Parmesan cheese, baking powder, ½ cup bacon bits and salt. In another bowl combine corn, eggs, sour cream, and oil, mixing well. Pour corn mixture into corn meal mixture. Pour ½ into greased 8-inch round cake pan. Sprinkle ¾ cup Cheddar cheese and remaining half of bacon bits on top of batter, then add remaining batter. Spread to cover to sides of pan. Sprinkle remaining cheese on top. Bake in 350° oven for 50 minutes.

## Macaroni and Cheese

*1 (8 ounce) package macaroni*
*1 can mushroom soup*
*1 (4 ounce) can mushroom pieces, drained*
*3/4 pound sharp Cheddar cheese, grated*
*1/4 can evaporated milk*
*1 stick margarine or butter*

Cook macaroni according to directions, drain, but do not rinse. Add all other ingredients, then bake in 350° oven for 30 minutes.

"For God has not given me
a spirit of fear, but of power, love
and of sound mind."
(II Timothy 1:7)

# Mandarin Salad

*1 teaspoon salt*
*¾ teaspoon coarsely ground black or white pepper*
*3 tablespoons sugar*
*4 tablespoons red wine vinegar*
*½-¾ teaspoon red pepper sauce*
*2 teaspoons parsley, finely chopped*
*½ cup salad oil*
*¾ cup sliced almonds*
*5-6 tablespoons sugar*
*½ head iceberg lettuce*
*½ head romaine lettuce*
*5 green onions (with tops) thinly sliced*
*2½ (11 ounce) cans chilled Mandarin orange segments*

Combine salt, pepper, 3 tablespoons sugar, red wine vinegar, red pepper sauce, parsley and salad oil. Shake well and chill. Cook almonds and sugar over low heat, stirring constantly, until sugar is melted and almonds are coated. Cool and break apart. Keep at room temperature. Tear lettuce into bite-sized pieces and toss with onions. Just before serving toss lettuce with ½ of the dressing. Drain Mandarin oranges, then add oranges and almonds to lettuce. Toss with remainder of dressing.

## Pimento Cheese Spread

- 2 (8 ounce) packages sharp Cheddar cheese, shredded
- 1 (4 ounce) jar diced pimento, undrained
- 1 cup mayonnaise
- ½ cup pecans, toasted and chopped
- ¼ teaspoon hot sauce

Stir together all ingredients; cover and chill at least 2 hours. Serve with crackers, use as a filling for a sandwich, or stuff celery with the pimento cheese.

*I especially like it with the celery.*

# Pumpkin Cheesecake

**Crust**

- ¾ *cup graham cracker crumbs*
- ½ *cup ground pecans*
- 2 *tablespoons sugar*
- 2 *tablespoons brown sugar*
- ¼ *cup margarine, melted*

Combine crust ingredients; mix well. Firmly press mixture into 9-inch springform cake pan.

**Filling**

- ¾ *cup sugar*
- ¾ *cup canned pumpkin*
- 3 *egg yolks*
- 1½ *teaspoons ground cinnamon*
- ½ *teaspoon ground mace*
- ½ *teaspoon ground ginger*
- ¼ *teaspoon salt*
- 3 *(8 ounce) packages cream cheese, softened*
- ¼ *cup plus 2 tablespoons sugar*
- 1 *egg*
- 2 *tablespoons whipping cream*
- 1 *tablespoon cornstarch*
- ½ *teaspoon vanilla extract*
- ½ *teaspoon lemon extract*
- *Whipped cream*
- *Pecan halves*

Combine ¾ cup sugar, pumpkin, 3 egg yolks, spices and salt in a medium bowl; mix well and set aside. Beat cream cheese with electric mixer until light and fluffy; gradually add ¼ cup plus 2 tablespoons sugar, mixing well. Add egg and whipping cream, beating well. Add cornstarch and flavorings; beat until smooth. Add pumpkin mixture; mix well. Pour into prepared pan. Bake at 350° for 50 to 55 minutes. Center may be soft but will firm when chilled. Let cool; chill thoroughly. Garnish with whipped cream and pecans.

# Sauerkraut Salad

*1 large jar or bag of sauerkraut*
*1 medium red bell pepper, chopped*
*1 medium green bell pepper, chopped*
*1 cup celery, chopped*
*1 medium onion, finely chopped*
*½ cup vinegar*
*¼ cup salad oil*
*1 cup sugar*
*Salt and pepper to taste (optional)*

Rinse sauerkraut several times in cold water; drain well. Make dressing with vinegar, oil and sugar. Combine all ingredients and place in covered container. Place in refrigerator at least overnight before serving. This is a great salad.

*One cup thinly sliced carrots is a nice addition to this salad.*

"The joy of the Lord is my strength."
(Nehemiah 8:10)

## Seafood Rosemary

- ½ *stick butter*
- 1 *cup milk*
- 2 *cups half & half*
- 1¼ *cups American cheese, diced*
- 1¼ *cups sharp Cheddar cheese, diced*
- 1 *pound shrimp, shelled and cleaned*
- ½ *pound cod fish, diced*
- 1 *pound small scallops*
- 1 *(1 pound) package imitation crabmeat, diced into ½-inch pieces*
- 2 *teaspoons garlic, minced*
- *Salt to taste*
- ⅔ *tablespoon cornstarch*
- ½ *cup cold milk*
- ½ *cup cooking wine (optional)*
- *Hot pepper sauce (optional)*

In a large, heavy pot, melt butter over medium heat. Slowly add milk and cream, stirring constantly. Pour cheese into milk mixture and stir as it melts. Add seafood, garlic and salt and continue stirring. Add cooking wine, if desired. Hot pepper sauce can be added to individual soup cups if desired. Good served with hot French or Italian bread.

*We serve this hearty dish a couple of hours before Christmas dinner, especially for those too hungry to wait! Serve in soup tureen then ladle into individual soup cups.*

## My Daddy

I had a wonderful daddy,
The greatest to ever walk the earth.
He thought that I was perfect,
From the first moment of my birth.

We shared almost everything.
He guided me, encouraged me,
And protected me in every possible way.
He carried me when I was tired,
Kissed away my hurts and dried my tears.

As I grew older he encouraged me in every way,
And his trust was complete.
I nearly broke his heart when I grew up and married,
Until he finally realized that I would always be his "little girl."

I wish that every child could have a daddy like mine,
But I am sure that God made only a
few as precious as "My Daddy."

*Jeannine Browning*

## Southern Pecan Pie

*3/4 stick butter*
*3/4 cup sugar*
*4 large eggs*
*1 1/4 cups white Karo syrup*
*2 cups pecans, chopped or halves*
*Pinch of salt*
*1 (10 inch) pie crust*

Melt butter in skillet. Add sugar and eggs, one at a time, beating well after each addition. Add Karo syrup and pecans. Pour into pie crust and place in 375° oven and bake for 35 to 45 minutes. Remove from oven and cool before cutting.

"I will never leave you or forsake you."
(Hebrews 13:5)

## Kumquat Pie

1 *quart ripe kumquats*
2 *cups orange juice*
1¼ *cups sugar*
2 *tablespoons flour*
2 *eggs, beaten*
2 *tablespoons margarine or butter*
*Top and bottom pie crust*

Slice and remove seeds from kumquats. Cover with orange juice and cook until tender and thick, then cool.

Mix all ingredients together and put in unbaked pie crust (about a 9 inch). Cover with top crust and bake at 375° for 1 hour.

*Make your own pie crust or buy from the grocery store.*

## Strawberry Salad

- 1 (6 ounce) package strawberry gelatin
- 1 cup boiling water
- 2 (10 ounce) packages frozen strawberries, sliced and thawed
- 1 (20 ounce) can crushed pineapple
- 3 medium bananas, mashed
- 1 cup walnuts, coarsely chopped
- 1 (8 ounce) carton sour cream

Dissolve gelatin in boiling water in a large bowl. Immediately add strawberries with juice, drained pineapple, bananas and walnuts. Pour ½ of strawberry mixture into a 13x9x2-inch dish. Refrigerate until nearly set. Spread sour cream evenly over gelatin. Gently spoon on rest of strawberry mixture; refrigerate until ready to serve. Cut and serve on lettuce leaf.

## Sweet Potato Soufflé

- 3 *cups sweet potatoes (yams), mashed*
- 1 *cup sugar*
- ½ *teaspoon salt (optional)*
- ⅓ *stick margarine, melted*
- ½ *cup milk*
- 2 *eggs, beaten*
- 1 *teaspoon butter flavoring*
- 1 *tablespoon orange juice*

Mix all ingredients and pour into baking dish. Cover with topping.

**Topping**

- 1 *cup brown sugar*
- ⅓ *cup flour*
- 1 *cup pecans, chopped*
- ⅓ *stick margarine*

Mix thoroughly and sprinkle over soufflé. Bake at 350° for 35 minutes.

*This is a real winner!*

# Turkey and Dressing

*1 (15 to 25 pound) turkey, fresh or frozen*

Place turkey in large baking pan with 2 to 3-inch sides. Sprinkle lightly with salt. Remove all hidden pieces in turkey...inside the turkey and under the neck flap. Either throw away or cook in water to cover, to use for broth or gravy. Cover turkey completely with aluminum foil to seal pan. Approximately 8 hours before you need your oven to bake other Christmas dishes, place defrosted or fresh turkey in oven on bottom rack and bake at 275°.

*A 15 pound turkey will take less time. We always need the 25 to 27 pound turkeys.*

**Cornbread**

*4 cups water-ground corn meal*
*4 eggs, beaten*
*2 heaping teaspoons baking powder*
*1 cup all-purpose flour*
*1 cup milk (approximately)*

Combine water-ground corn meal, eggs, baking powder, flour and milk. Mix well, pour into greased baking pan. Bake at 450° for about 30 minutes. Cool. Break cornbread into small pieces and place in a large mixing bowl.

*3 teaspoons sage, crumbled*
*2 large onions, finely chopped*
*1 large bag seasoned breadcrumbs*
*8 eggs, beaten*
*1 teaspoon red hot dried pepper, finely chopped (optional)*
*6 cups broth, or more if needed*

Combine all ingredients. Batter must be juicy before cooking. Add broth from cooked turkey to enhance flavor. Place in baking pans, baking on broil, with oven door slightly open. Stir as top browns. Keep stirring until dressing is at desired texture...not too juicy and definitely not too dry.

*Once you try this recipe you won't want any other dressing. About half our family likes our dressing as hot as can be, and the other half likes it very mild. Therefore, I divide the dressing and fix some mild and some very hot. Gravy is a necessity for some of us.*

# Yellow Squash Casserole

*2 pounds yellow squash, sliced*
*2 large carrots, scraped and grated*
*1 large onion, finely chopped*
*1 can cream of chicken soup*
*1 (2 ounce) jar pimento, chopped*
*1 (8 ounce) package Pepperidge Farm herb dressing*
*1 cup sour cream*
*1 teaspoon salt*
*1/4 teaspoon pepper*
*1 stick margarine, melted*
*Paprika*

Boil squash, carrots and onion in water to cover. Drain well and mash. Add soup, pimento, sour cream, salt and pepper and mix well. Combine margarine with herb dressing. Sprinkle ½ of dressing mixture in buttered 2½-quart casserole dish. Pour squash mixture over and top with remaining dressing. Sprinkle with paprika and bake at 350° for 1 hour.

*The Christmas meal, whether at noon or later in the day, is always a very special one. We always have turkey and dressing with gravy, Sweet Potato Soufflé, vegetables, salads, roasted pecans and lots of desserts. Try to choose a few dishes that can be prepared in advance. I always make the corn bread for the corn bread dressing at least a few days before Christmas and freeze. Remove from the freezer a few hours before using. I also make my salads a few days before Christmas. Do as many things in advance as you can, because if you are anything like me, I want to be in the living room with the rest of the family when all the gifts are opened. Set your tables the night before, if you can. Enjoy a special and blessed day.*

# The Day After Christmas

# Butterflies

Children are like butterflies
Flitting here and there,
They represent God's beauty
That fills the very air.

They are so very precious
These special gifts from God,
They grow up oh so quickly,
Just close your eyes and nod.

Take time to enjoy your children
These precious, fragile souls,
Just give them love and compassion,
And encouragement to attain life's goals.

Children are like butterflies
So beautiful to see,
These special gifts from God
Mean everything to me.

J. Browning

## Beef Parmesan

*1½ pounds good round steak*
*½ cup grated Parmesan cheese*
*⅓ cup breadcrumbs*
*2 eggs, beaten*
*⅓ cup vegetable oil*
*1 medium-sized onion, chopped*
*1 teaspoon salt*
*¼ teaspoon pepper*
*1 teaspoon sugar*
*½ teaspoon marjoram*
*Garlic to taste (about 3 cloves)*
*1 (6 ounce) can tomato paste*
*1 cup hot water*
*1 (8 ounce) package mozzarella cheese slices*
*Buttered noodles*

Place meat between 2 pieces of wax paper, lay on cutting board and pound thin. Cut into thin, small bite-sized pieces. Mix Parmesan cheese and breadcrumbs. Dip meat in beaten eggs and roll in breadcrumbs.

Heat oil and brown steak. Place in baking dish. Cook onion until soft in skillet in which meat was browned. Stir in seasonings and tomato paste. Add hot water and stir. Pour part of sauce over meat, top with cheese slices and add remaining sauce. Bake at 350° for 1 hour.

*Kevin (my son) heats some prepared spaghetti sauce and spoons it over the noodles before adding the Beef Parmesan. This is one of our favorite recipes. Great to prepare in advance and freeze. If you plan to freeze it, cook for 45 minutes instead of 1 hour. When ready to serve, thaw and cook about 30 minutes. Serves 4 to 6.*

## Cajun Turkey Gumbo

*1 cup cooked ham, diced*
*1 cup onion, finely chopped*
*¼ cup margarine*
*2 (1 pound) cans whole tomatoes, drained*
*1 (6 ounce) can tomato paste*
*2 cloves garlic, crushed*
*2 teaspoons salt*
*1 bay leaf*
*½ teaspoon black pepper*
*½ teaspoon crumbled basil*
*¼ teaspoon hot pepper sauce*
*¼ teaspoon chili powder*
*¼ teaspoon leaf thyme*
*1 (10 ounce) package frozen okra, sliced*
*½ pound (1 cup) shelled shrimp, fresh or frozen*
*2 cups cooked turkey, cut into bite sized pieces*
*4 cups cooked rice*

Sauté onion and ham in butter for 4 minutes. Remove from heat. Combine tomatoes, tomato paste, garlic, salt, bay leaf, pepper, basil, hot pepper sauce, chili powder and leaf thyme. Add tomato mixture to onion and ham in large, heavy pan. Bring to a boil. Stir in okra and shrimp. Reduce heat and cook covered, stirring once or twice, for 10 minutes. Add turkey and cook 2 minutes longer. Serve in soup bowl with a large spoonful of cooked rice in each bowl.

# The Day After Christmas

"And we know that all things work out together for good, for those who love God, for those who are called according to His Purpose."
(Romans 8:28)

## Cornbread Biscuits with Cheese and Sesame Seeds

- 5 *tablespoons sesame seeds (cooked for 2 minutes in heavy skillet and cooled)*
- 2½ *cups all-purpose flour*
- 4 *teaspoons baking powder*
- ¾ *teaspoon salt*
- ½ *teaspoon baking soda*
- ½ *cup yellow corn meal*
- ¼ *stick chilled butter, cut into small pieces*
- 1½ *cups buttermilk*
- 4 *teaspoons fresh sage, chopped (or 1½ teaspoons dried sage)*
- 1 *tablespoon fresh thyme (or 1 teaspoon dried thyme)*
- 2 *cups sharp Cheddar cheese, grated*
- ¼ *cup buttermilk*

Mix flour, baking powder, salt and baking soda in large bowl. Add corn meal and 3 tablespoons sesame seeds and stir. Add chilled butter and blend in with fingertips until mixed well. Whisk 1½ cups buttermilk, chopped sage and thyme in medium-sized bowl. Add to dry ingredients and stir well. Add cheese. Dough will be slightly sticky. Form into a ball and turn out on a well-floured surface. Knead dough a few times, adding more flour if dough is still sticky. Roll out to ¼ or ½-inch thickness and cut with a round biscuit or cookie cutter. Place on ungreased baking sheets. Brush with additional buttermilk and sprinkle top with remaining 2 teaspoons toasted sesame seeds. Bake 16 minutes in 350° oven.

*This is great with dried bean and ham soup. If you have leftover ham from Christmas, just buy a package of Great Northern dried beans and soak in water to cover overnight or at least 6 hours. Drain off all water. Add more water to cover, 2 finely chopped onions and your left over ham, including bone. Cook for 4 to 6 hours, stirring every hour or so. This will be a great meal with your Cornmeal Biscuits and a salad.*

# Your Favorite Memories

## Ham-Mushroom Tomato Quiche

*1 prepared 9-inch pie crust, unbaked*
*¾-1 cup cooked ham, diced*
*1 cup American or sharp Cheddar cheese, diced or grated*
*3 eggs, well beaten*
*½-¾ cup whole milk or half & half*
*1 teaspoon salt*
*1 tablespoon onion, finely chopped*
*1 cup fresh mushrooms, sliced*

In a large bowl combine above ingredients and pour into prepared pie crust.

*1-2 large tomatoes, thinly sliced*
*Fresh or dried parsley*
*1 tablespoon butter*

Preheat oven to 350°. Thinly slice tomatoes and place whole round slices on top of mixture. Sprinkle with parsley on top and dot with butter. Bake for 45 minutes to 1 hour. Quiche is done when a table knife is inserted in center and comes out clean. Cool a few minutes, then slice and serve. When completely cool it can be covered and placed in the refrigerator and reheated the next day.

## Hearty Taco Soup

- 2 *pounds lean ground beef (or ground turkey)*
- 1 *large onion, finely chopped*
- 1 *(4 ounce) can chopped green chiles (optional)*
- 1 *teaspoon salt*
- 1 *teaspoon pepper*
- 1 *(16 ounce) can pinto beans, drained*
- 1 *(16 ounce) can lima beans, drained*
- 1 *(22 ounce) can red kidney beans, drained*
- 1 *(15¼ ounce) can whole corn, drained*
- 1 *envelope taco seasoning mix*
- 4 *cups water*
- 1 *envelope ranch dressing mix*
- 2 *(15 ounce) cans stewed tomatoes*

*Shredded Cheddar cheese*
*Tortilla chips*

Brown beef or turkey with onions; drain. Add next 11 ingredients. Simmer for 30 to 45 minutes. Garnish with Cheddar cheese and chips.

"It is a good thing to give thanks unto the Lord."
(Psalm 92:1)

# Jello Salad

2 *(3 ounce) packages lemon jello*
2 *cups boiling water*
2 *cups Sprite or 7-Up*
2 *cups miniature marshmallows*
1 *cup crushed pineapple, drained, save juice*
3-4 *bananas, sliced*

Dissolve jello in water; add Sprite or 7-Up. Add other ingredients and mix well. Pour into large rectangular serving dish. Chill until firm.

**Topping**

½ *cup sugar*
2 *tablespoons flour*
1 *cup pineapple juice (if not enough juice, add water to make 1 cup)*
2 *eggs, beaten*
1 *cup (or more) Cool Whip*

Combine sugar, flour, juice and eggs. Stir over low heat until thick. Chill. Fold in Cool Whip until well mixed and spread on top of jello mixture.

## Lasagna - Spinach Casserole

- ½ *cup onion, finely chopped or grated*
- 1 *clove garlic, chopped*
- 2 *pounds lean ground beef*
- 2 *tablespoons salad oil, divided*
- 2 *teaspoons salt*
- 4 *(8 ounce) cans tomato sauce*
- 1 *(6 ounce) can tomato paste*
- 1 *teaspoon oregano*
- 2 *(3 ounce) jars mushrooms, sliced*
- 2 *eggs, divided*
- 1 *(8 ounce) package lasagna noodles, cooked and drained*
- 1 *package frozen spinach, chopped, cooked and drained*
- 1 *cup Parmesan cheese, grated*
- ½ *pint small curd cottage cheese*
- 1 *package American cheese slices*

Brown onion, garlic and ground beef in 1 tablespoon salad oil; season with 1 teaspoon salt. Set aside. Combine tomato sauce, tomato paste, oregano and mushrooms. Simmer for 15 minutes. Beat 1 egg slightly; pour over cooked noodles. Beat second egg and combine with spinach, 1 tablespoon salad oil, 1 teaspoon salt and Parmesan cheese. Pour half the tomato mixture in a 15x10x2-inch baking pan. Cover with ½ the noodles. Add spinach mixture and cottage cheese; cover with remaining noodles. Add meat; cover with remaining tomato mixture. Cover pan with foil. Bake at 350° for 1 hour. Five minutes before done, remove foil and cover with American cheese. Bake until cheese is melted. Cut into squares to serve.

## Mushroom Sauce for Steaks

- 1 *quart of thickly sliced mushrooms*
- ½ *stick margarine or butter*
- ¼ *cup balsamic vinegar*
- 3 *tablespoons Worcestershire sauce*
- 1 *tablespoon soy sauce*
- 2-3 *tablespoons sugar*

Sauté mushrooms in melted butter until browned, then add remaining ingredients. Cook to about 50% reduction of sauce. Serve hot over meat.

"Man shall not live by bread alone,
but by every word that proceeds from
the mouth of God."
(Matthew 4:4)

Just as we need to partake of food daily
to be physically strong, we need to meditate on
God's word daily to be spiritually strong.

## Smoked Turkey Breast Sandwich

*8 slices smoked turkey breast*
*4 slices pumpernickel bread*
*Mayonnaise*
*4 slices Muenster cheese*
*4 tablespoons toasted, slivered almonds*
*¾ cup peach chutney*

Lightly spread each slice of bread with mayonnaise. Layer with two large slices smoked turkey, then cheese. Sprinkle with toasted almonds. Broil 4 to 5 minutes until cheese melts and bubbles. Remove from oven and generously cover each sandwich with peach chutney, about 2 to 3 tablespoons. Serve warm.

# Sweet Romaine and Walnut Salad

**Noodles**

1 *tablespoon butter*
1 *package Ramen noodles (throw away seasoning packet)*
1 *cup walnuts, chopped*

Place 1 tablespoon butter in nonstick frying pan and melt. Add broken noodles and walnuts to butter and stir until lightly browned. Set aside.

**Salad**

2 *heads of hearts of romaine, broken into bite-sized pieces*
1 *package broccoli, cut into small pieces*
1 *bunch green onions, thinly sliced*

Toss and serve with the following dressing, then add noodles and walnuts and serve.

**Dressing**

½ *cup olive oil*
¼ *cup honey*
⅓ *cup white wine vinegar*
¼ *teaspoon each salt and pepper*

Combine well.

## Turkey Florentine Quiche

- 1 *prepared 9-inch pie crust, unbaked*
- ¼-½ *package frozen spinach, defrosted and cooked*
- ¾-1 *cup cooked turkey, diced*
- 1 *cup American or sharp Cheddar cheese, grated*
- 3 *eggs, well beaten*
- ½-¾ *cup whole milk or half & half*
- 1 *teaspoon salt*
- 1 *tablespoon curry powder (optional)*
- 1 *tablespoon onion, finely chopped*

Preheat oven to 350°. Mix all ingredients together and pour into prepared 9-inch pie crust. Bake for 45 minutes to 1 hour. Quiche is done when a table knife is inserted into center of quiche and comes out clean.

"You are my beloved Son; you are my Delight."
(Mark 1:11)

## The Lamb

"Tomorrow morning," the surgeon began, "I'll open up your heart..."

"You'll find Jesus there," the boy interrupted.

The surgeon looked up, annoyed. "I'll cut your heart open,' he continued, "to see how much damage has been done..."

"But when you open up my heart, you'll find Jesus in there."

The surgeon looked to the parents, who sat quietly. "When I see how much damage has been done, I'll sew your heart and chest back up and I'll plan what to do next."

"But you'll find Jesus in my heart. The Bible says He lives there. The hymns all say He lives there. You'll find Him in my heart."

The surgeon had had enough. "I'll tell you what I'll find in your heart. I'll find damaged muscle, low blood supply, and weakened vessels. And I'll find out if I can make you well."

"You'll find Jesus there, too. He lives there."

The surgeon left.

The surgeon sat in his office, recording his note from the surgery, "damaged aorta, damaged pulmonary vein, widespread muscle degeneration. No hope for transplant, no hope for cure.

Therapy: painkillers and bed rest.

Prognosis: here he paused, "death within one year."

He stopped the recorder, but there was more to be said.

"Why?" he asked aloud. "Why did You do this? You've put him here; You've put him in this pain; and You've cursed him to an early death.

Why?"

The Lord answered and said, "The boy, My lamb, was not meant for your flock for long, for he is a part of My flock, and will forever be. Here, in My flock, he will feel no pain, and will be comforted as you cannot imagine. His parents will one day join him here, and they will know peace, and My flock will continue to grow."

The surgeon's tears were hot, but his anger was hotter. "You created that boy, and You created that heart. He'll be dead in months. Why?"

The Lord answered. "The boy, My lamb, shall return to My flock, for he has done his duty: I did not put My lamb with your flock to lose him, but to retrieve another lost lamb."

The surgeon wept.

The surgeon sat beside the boy's bed; the boy's parents sat across from him.

The boy awoke and whispered, "Did you cut open my heart?"

"Yes", said the surgeon.

"What did you find?" asked the boy.

"I found Jesus there," said the surgeon.

*Author unknown*

# Rosemary Fry (Ossenfort) Brofos

Rosemary Fry (Ossenfort) Brofos, the talented artist for Christmas Memories, was born in Chicago, Illinois. Her growing up years were divided between Chicago and Kissimmee, Florida.

Rosemary has three children, one grandson, three grandchildren through her children's spouses and one step-grandson.

Rosemary is a Marriage and Family Therapist with a Masters degree. She and husband, Frederick, are now retired, spending summers in New Hampshire and winters in Florida.

# Index

## A



## B

# Index

# Index

## E

# Index

# Index

## S

# Index

# *Cookbooks by Jeannine*

8552 Sylvan Drive
Melbourne, Florida 32904-2426
Telephone: (321) 723-5111
Fax: (321) 725-3354

Please send ____ copies of *Christmas Memories* .......... @ $22.95 each ______

Please send ____ copies of *Sand In My Shoes* ............ @ 14.95 each ______

Please send ____ copies of *Florida Fixin's* .................... @ 12.95 each ______

Please send ____ copies of *Kids At Work* ........................ @ 12.95 each ______

Florida residents add 6% sales tax ........................................................ ______

Add UPS and handling ...................................................... @ 2.50 each ______

Total ____________

❑ Check or money order enclosed. (Make checks payable to *Cookbooks by Jeannine*.)

Please charge to: ❑ MasterCard ❑ Visa ❑ Discover

Card Number: ______________________________________________

Expiration Date: ___________ Signature: ______________________________

From:

Name ______________________________________________

Address ______________________________________________

City ______________________________________________

State ________________________________ Zip ________________

Ship To:

Name ______________________________________________

Address ______________________________________________

City ______________________________________________

State ________________________________ Zip ________________

Phone Number ( ) ________________________

(No P.O. Boxes)